The Rise and Fall of Economic Growth

To D.M.B. and R.M.S.

The Rise and Fall of Economic Growth
Growth
A Study in Contemporary Thought

H.W. Arndt

Longman Cheshire

Longman Cheshire Pty Limited
346 St Kilda Road
Melbourne Australia 3004

Offices in Sydney, Brisbane, Adelaide, and
Perth. Associated companies, branches, and
representatives throughout the world.

First published 1978

Printed in Singapore by Kua Co., Book Manufacturer, Pte Ltd.

National Library of Australia
Cataloguing-in-Publication data

Arndt, Heinz Wolfgang, 1915 —.
   The rise and fall of economic growth.

   Index.
   ISBN 0 582 71213 0 Paperback
   ISBN 0 582 71214 9

   1. Economics. I. Title.

330.1

Contents

1 Introductory

The object of this study is to describe and explain the rise of 'economic growth' to pre-eminence among policy objectives in western countries between 1945 and 1965, and the attack on this objective from various quarters in the past decade.

A few preliminary explanations are needed.

We shall not be concerned with what economists call growth *theory*, that is the body of theory which attempts, through abstract models with or without supporting empirical evidence, to explain the process of economic growth; nor with economic history, the study of how and why economic change occurred in particular periods and parts of the world; nor with philosophy of history, the search for broad generalisations or fundamental laws of historical evolution.

The study will focus on changing views about the relative importance of economic growth as an objective of policy, as contrasted with such other objectives as stability or equality or freedom or national power. Policy never aims at just one objective; even a dictator, relatively untrammelled by pressures from warring factions, has to choose his preferred mix of objectives. What we shall be concerned with is changing views about the desirable mix — the most appropriate trade-off, in contemporary economists' jargon — between economic growth and other objectives.

By 'economic growth' we shall mean growth in average or per capita income (commonly measured by a country's Gross Domestic Product, GDP, divided by its population) rather than growth of total GDP. In other words, we are interested in what nineteenth century writers called 'material progress' and what people nowadays have in mind when they speak of 'rising living standards', rather than in population growth. But we shall find that we cannot entirely ignore population growth because some of the most serious problems

1

facing the world today are the joint product of economic growth and population growth.

This relative unconcern with population growth may be excusable because we shall concentrate almost exclusively on the rich or developed countries. (With an apologetic bow towards Tokyo, we shall frequently, for simplicity, call them the 'western' countries.) We shall therefore almost entirely neglect the Second and Third Worlds, not because the issues are irrelevant to them but because they need different treatment, in the developing countries of the Third World because in relation to most of them the need for higher per capita incomes hardly can be disputed, and in the communist countries of the Second World because its desirability (like much else) never is disputed. It is clearly in relation to the countries in which living standards are already high that the case for economic growth is most debatable.

The study will be an essay in the history of thought, but if economics is concerned with means not ends — a famous definition defines its subject matter as the relationship between ends and scarce means which have alternative uses — not in the history of *economic* thought. According to this definition, the choice of ends of policy, the optimum mix of economic growth, stability, equality, power and freedom, involves value judgments about which the science of economics as such has nothing to say. Others have expressed doubt whether ends and means can be so sharply distinguished. Be that as it may, we shall draw very largely on the writings of professional economists, academic and other, for evidence on the rise and fall of economic growth as a policy objective.

The reason is simply that economists have most to say on the subject. Whenever they think or write about economic policy, about the most appropriate means, they must make explicit or implicit assumptions about ends, about the specific objectives, or mix of objectives, which governments have announced or which public opinion is believed to favour or which they personally think desirable. Often economists will make their assumptions explicit, if only in the first or last paragraphs of a technical treatise or article. (This is one reason why some economists quoted in later chapters may feel that undue weight has been given to what were really *obiter dicta*. Most of these will still be rather better evidence of serious contemporary thought than casual pronouncements of journalists, politicians or public opinion polls.)

It is true that in the chapters on the Fall we shall have more frequent occasion to draw on the writings of non-economists than in those on the Rise, a fact which may seem to lend support to the popular view that economists have a professional bias in favour of economic growth. An alternative explanation is that more economists are employed or employ themselves in the study of the best means of achieving than of frustrating the objectives favoured by majority or dominant opinion at any time. We shall see that the most trenchant and articulate critics of the economic growth objective were also economists.

This, of course, is also why economics is more subject to what looks like changes of fashion than other sciences, though the difference is only a matter of degree. Economists, like physicists and biologists, prefer to study problems which are interesting and important. Sometimes — and more commonly in mathematics than in physics, biology or philosophy and more often in any of these than in economics, but also perhaps more often in economics than in the less rigorous social sciences — a problem is interesting or important because it represents a puzzle or gap in the logical coherence of a body of theory. But in economics it is usually its relevance to the concerns of people — governments, interest groups, voters — in the real world that lends interest or importance to a problem. Economic growth became fashionable in economics in the post-1945 period partly as economists followed up the internal logic of Keynesian macroeconomics, but mainly and decisively because, for reasons which it is the purpose of chapters three to five of this book to examine, governments, interest groups and voters in western countries came to attach greater weight to economic growth as an objective of national policy.

Two further limitations of this study need to be pointed out. First, and most regrettably, the evidence is drawn almost entirely from writings in the English language. (And even among these, readers may be surprised, in view of the author's citizenship, to note a complete absence of references to Australian writings. The reason is that there was originally to be a chapter on the Australian case, with its interesting special nuances; this will now have to be a separate piece.) The neglect of the thought of the countries of continental Europe and Japan is serious for chapter two on the 'Pre-History', for in all these countries, determined to catch up, economic development remained in the foreground as a major objective of national policy even during the period 1870 to 1914 when it was tacitly taken for granted in Britain and the United States. The neglect probably matters a good deal less for the post-1945 period when attitudes to economic growth do not seem to have diverged very greatly between English-speaking and other 'western' countries.

Secondly, the evidence is drawn entirely from writings, by economists and others, not from statistics, because it focuses on what was sought rather than what was achieved. There is ample statistical evidence that the developed countries achieved on average a higher rate of economic growth during the two decades of the 1950s and 1960s than had ever been attained before in modern, and probably in all, history. There are also increasing signs that the average rate of economic growth in these countries has slowed down markedly during the 1970s. How far the acceleration of economic growth in the post-1945 years was the *result* of deliberate policy, under the influence of a shift of opinion in favour of economic growth as a policy objective; how far the slowdown in economic growth during recent years reflects policy changes under the influence of a climate of opinion less favourable to economic growth; and what role the writings of economists surveyed in subsequent chapters have played in bringing about changes in the climate of opinion and in policies — these are matters which it would take a different book to examine. Almost certainly, changes in opinion and policy have played some part in both the acceleration and the deceleration, though both have in part been the product of historical forces, economic and political, willed by no one. Similarly, the writings of economists have almost certainly been influential, but more in reflecting and articulating and perhaps here and there leading shifts of opinion, rather than in bringing them about.

Thought about the desirability of economic growth relative to other objectives of economic policy leads inevitably to happiness, justice, freedom and all the other unanswerable questions about man and society and the universe. A modest essay in the history of thought will not be expected to answer the unanswerable. The last chapter attempts no more than a little sorting out of the wheat from the chaff. Its object is to advance not to end the debate.

2 The Pre-History

The idea of material progress as a possible or desirable human condition does not, in western thought, go back much beyond the beginning of the eighteenth century. Medieval man, expecting little from his brief span in this vale of tears, sought — or at any rate was urged to seek — the salvation of his soul. The new age of rational and scientific enquiry which began with the Renaissance led daring minds to envisage the possibility of continuing progress, but for long the emphasis was on progress of knowledge. Francis Bacon, with his utilitarian view of 'the endowment of human life with new inventions *and riches*' as the real and legitimate goal of the sciences, was well ahead of his time.[1] It was not until the first decades of the eighteenth century that precursors of the French enlightenment, such as Abbe de Saint-Pierre, gave the idea of progress a specifically economic facet.[2]

The reason why the idea of economic progress was so late in coming was put very simply by Keynes when, in 1930, to counter the bad attack of economic pessimism of those years, he wrote about 'Economic Possibilities for our Grandchildren':

> From the earliest times of which we have record — back, say, to two thousand years before Christ — down to the beginning of the eighteenth century, there was no very great change in the standard of life of the average man living in the civilised centres of the earth. Ups and downs certainly. Visitations of plague, famine, and war. Golden intervals. But no progressive violent change. Some periods perhaps 50 per cent better than others — at the utmost 100 per cent better — in the four thousand years which ended (say) in A.D. 1700... This slow rate of progress, or lack of progress, was due to two reasons — to the remarkable absence of important technical improvements and to the failure of capital to accumulate.[3]

Even utopia must be conceivable. People did not begin to think of material progress as desirable until events proved that it was possible.

Mercantilism

The first two centuries of the modern age — which Keynes thought began in the sixteenth century with the inflation caused in Europe by inflow of gold and silver from the new world — were the period of emerging nation states. Capitalism progressed under the tutelage, for their own purposes, of absolute monarchs. Governments consciously fostered economic development, but the object was not so much rising living standards as national strength — kings 'bowing', in the words of Bacon's comment on the imposition by Henry VII of duties on imports of wine from France, 'the policy of this estate, from consideration of plenty to consideration of power'.[4] How little the mercantilists were concerned with rising living standards is nicely illustrated by a passage from Sir James Steuart's *Principles:* 'We must encourage oeconomy, frugality, and a simplicity of manners, discourage the consumption of every thing that can be exported, and excite a taste for superfluity in neighbouring nations.'[5]

Sir James's more worldly contemporary, David Hume, criticised the mercantilist doctrine, partly because he believed that foreign trade would promote economic development by creating new wants:

If we consult history, we shall find that, in most nations, foreign trade has preceded any refinement in home manufactures, and given birth to domestic luxury. The temptation is stronger to make use of foreign commodities... Thus men become acquainted with the *pleasures* of luxury and the *profits* of commerce; and their *delicacy* and *industry*, being once awakened, carry them on to further improvements, in every branch of domestic as well as foreign trade. And this perhaps is the chief advantage which arises from a commerce with strangers. It rouses men from their indolence; and presenting the gayer and more opulent part of the nation with objects of luxury which they never before dreamed of, raises in them a desire of a more splendid way of life than what their ancestors enjoyed.

But Hume's conclusion was still a mercantilist one: 'When the affairs of the society are once brought to this situation, a nation may lose most of its foreign trade, and yet continue a great and powerful people.'[6]

The Classical Economists

'The progressive state is in reality the cheerful and the hearty state to all the different orders of the society. The stationary state is dull; the declining melancholy.'[7] Although Adam Smith made this statement in the context of a rather technical argument — that real wages can be above subsistence level only while the stock of capital and the demand for labour are growing — he was speaking from the heart. By the mid-eighteenth century, at least in the British Isles, the conviction had grown that economic progress was possible and desirable, as a source not merely of national power but of the prosperity of the people, and that further economic progress demanded the emancipation of trade and industry from government control; *laissez faire*!

> In the midst of all the exactions of government, this capital has been silently and gradually accumulated by the private frugality and good conduct of individuals, by their universal, continual, and uninterrupted effort to better their own condition. It is this effort...which has maintained the progress of England towards opulence and improvement in almost all former times, and which, it is to be hoped, will do so in all future times.[8]

No doubt, the merchants, bankers and manufacturers of England and Scotland interpreted 'progress' and 'prosperity' in their own light. But to a professor of moral philosophy the answer to the question whether improvement in the circumstances of the lower ranks of the people was to be regarded as an advantage or as an inconvenience to the society was plain: 'No society can surely be flourishing and happy, of which the far greater part of the members are poor and miserable.'[9]

The classical economists from Adam Smith to Ricardo rarely expatiated on the desirability of material progress because they took it for granted. They agreed, by and large, with the French encyclopaedists and the English utilitarians that the object of government was the happiness of the people and that material progress was conclusive to this end, though none of them would have subscribed to this view in the crude version of Mercier de la Rivière: 'The greatest happiness possible for us consists in the greatest possible abundance of objects suitable to our enjoyment and in the greatest liberty to profit by them.'[10] Their concern was to argue the case for the policies which, they believed, were needed to promote economic growth. It was this objective, rather than allocative efficiency, which inspired their advocacy of free trade. It was also this same 'deep-rooted belief that the economic welfare of society can be promoted in a far more far-reaching manner by expanding the total volume of its economic activity than by accepting its available resources as given and trying to allocate them more efficiently among different industries'[11] that led them to develop the elements of a theory of economic growth and to speculate about the future of capitalism.

The 'magnificent dynamics' of the classical economists, which has been much discussed and dissected in recent years, is not strictly relevant to our purpose. But optimism or pessimism about the future of economic growth is liable to colour one's views about its desirability, and analysis of the process of economic growth may have implications for policy. A brief digression on classical growth theory, as exemplified by its chief exponents, may therefore be worthwhile.

Adam Smith, as we have seen, looked forward to 'the progress of England towards opulence and improvement...in all future times'. As yet unworried about population growth and diminishing returns, he really had no reason to fear that economic growth would ever stop. His main argument for expecting a declining rate of profit — that just as mutual competition among rich merchants in the same trade tends to lower its profit so, in the same society, 'the same competition must produce the same effect on them all' — was clearly fallacious. More than once he suggested that any country will, at some stage in the future, reach 'its full complement of riches', a phrase which seemed to imply a belief that growth must ultimately end in a stationary state because of the satiability of human wants. But in the one example he gave, China, the limits to growth seemed to be set in the long run by soil and climate, and in the meantime by laws and institutions:

> In a country which had acquired that full complement of riches which the nature of its soil and climate, and its situation with respect to other countries, allowed it to acquire; which could, therefore, advance no further...both the wages of labour and the profits of stock would probably be very low... Perhaps no country has yet arrived at this degree of opulence. China seems to have been long stationary, and had probably long ago acquired that full complement of riches that is consistent with the nature of its laws and institutions. But this complement may be much inferior to what, with other laws and institutions, the nature of its soil, climate and situation might admit of.[12]

The last decade of the eighteenth century and the first two of the nineteenth were a time of trouble in England — war against revolutionary and imperial France, deteriorating social conditions in the growing industrial cities and serious unemployment in the post-war depression. The troubles were reflected in the much less optimistic outlook of the second generation of classical economists. Malthus, although, as befits a clergyman, more concerned with man's moral than material progress, unquestionably shared Adam Smith's belief in the desirability of rising living standards, but he was fearful for the future. On the side of supply, rising living standards were threatened by population growth which, unless checked by moral restraint, was bound to outrun food supply. On the side of demand, prosperity was threatened by 'glut', due to excessive saving, which would 'leave no motive to a further increase in production'.[13]

Ricardo rejected the latter and modified the former ground for pessimism. He demonstrated to his own satisfaction, and that of the mainstream of economics for a hundred years, that Say's Law precludes the possibility of general overproduction; and his own reasons for expecting economic growth to end in a stationary state were much more sophisticated than crude Malthusianism. In the Ricardian model, the rate of profit on which the process of capital accumulation and economic growth depends, is bound to fall as the pressure of population on limited land transfers an increasing proportion of income as rent to landlords — *unless*, and to the extent that, this tendency is offset by technical progress and the opening up of new land overseas. Ricardo, too, believed in something like an iron law of wages, whereby population growth accelerates whenever real wages rise above subsistence level. But unlike Smith's formulation (and Malthus's earlier version) which seemed virtually to rule out a secular rise in real wages, Ricardo included in the labourer's subsistence minimum 'necessaries and conveniences become essential to him from habit',[14] thus permitting a rising subsistence minimum. Ricardo was no pessimist. 'His Stationary State...can be put off, by wise policy...into the almost indefinite future...by developing foreign trade, by the exploitation of the almost limitless resources of the extra-European world'[15] and, presumably, by technical progress.* Nor, the opening lines of

---

*This, surely, is a sounder assessment than Samuelson's view that Ricardo and Malthus 'represented a retreat from preoccupation with dynamic progress, retreat to a gloomy concentration upon the law of diminishing returns' (*Collected Scientific Papers* [MIT, Cambridge, Mass., 1966], vol. 3, p. 704).

the *Principles* notwithstanding, was Ricardo primarily interested in the distribution of a given national product among the social classes. He was concerned lest the redistribution in favour of landowners, which was liable to occur in the absence of wise policies, strangle economic growth by depressing the rate of profit.* That economic growth was desirable, in the interests of wage earners — 'by far the most important class in society'[16] — as of the capitalists, he never doubted.

Marx, for most of his life, was too preoccupied with proving the inevitability of the revolutionary overthrow of capitalism and with helping to bring it about to spell out the objectives of the society that was to follow. As an economist, Marx was a Ricardian who believed in the declining rate of profit but, since he rejected Malthusianism, had to prop up this belief with a variety of unconvincing arguments.[17] Unlike Engels, however, Marx was no utilitarian.[18] He had nothing but contempt for the devotees of material progress and of the greatest happiness for the greatest number. As a young Hegelian he had something to say about 'the abundance of human wants' under socialism, but as 'confirmation of man's creativeness and enrichment of his being', not of anything as vulgar as the standard of living.[19] And when a few years later, in the *Communist Manifesto*, he sang his famous hymn of praise to the achievements of capitalism — which has created 'more massive and more colossal productive forces than have all preceding generations together' — his focus was on the role of the bourgeoisie in creating urban civilisation, in rescuing 'a considerable part of the population from the idiocy of rural life',[20] rather than in growth of per capita income. If, as a young man, Marx had visualised communist society as an arcadian utopia without division of labour in which man hunts in the morning, fishes in the afternoon, rears cattle in the evening, and exercises his critical faculties at night,[21] he saw it nearly fifty years later, in his old age, no less romantically, as society composed of small co-operative communities in which, as in an Israeli kibbutz, 'a quite different distribution of consumer goods automatically follows':

---

*Here again, Samuelson seems to misinterpret Ricardo's position in his comment that 'once optimistic hopes of progressive growth were abandoned, it was natural for political economists like Ricardo to concentrate upon the distribution of the fixed national product among competing classes' (*Collected Scientific Papers* [MIT, Cambridge, Mass., 1966], vol. 3, p. 704).

In the higher phase of communist society, when the slavish sub-jection of the individual to the division of labour and the contrast between mental and physical labour have disappeared; when work itself is no longer merely a means to life but something that makes life worth living; when, with the all-round development of indi-viduals, their productive powers have grown and all the springs of co-operative (*genossenschaftlich*) wealth flow in abundance, only then can bourgeois justice be surpassed and society can inscribe on its banner: from each according to his ability, to each according to his need![22]

Marx was

simply not concerned to portray Communism as a society of plenty; he [was] concerned to portray it as a society of human dignity: a society in which labour acquires dignity and becomes free because it is carried out by full and conscious participants in a community given over to co-operation and common aims.[23]*

J.S. Mill

John Stuart Mill was in some ways less of a Ricardian than Marx, although he remained all his life almost as anxious to claim, as Marx was to disclaim, this intellectual parentage. Brought up by his father in the strict Benthamite school, he came, as he acknow-ledged in his *Autobiography*, to be much influenced by Coleridge and other critics of industrial capitalism. He became, as Schumpe-ter has pointed out, 'a man palpably out of sympathy with the scheme of values of the industrial bourgeoisie...an evolutionary socialist...[hardly] a utilitarian at all'.[24]

On the likelihood of future economic growth J.S. Mill had nothing very new to say. He accepted Ricardo's argument that the rate of profit would fall and accumulation sooner or later cease if population continued to grow and outran food supply. He also argued, unconvincingly, that this would happen even with a stationary population, in the absence of technical progress or unless 'other circumstances having a tendency to raise the rate of profit occurred in the meantime'.[25] But he gave many reasons for

---

*By contrast, Engels envisaged the post-capitalist utopia in terms of bigger and better economic growth: 'Crises will disappear; increased pro-duction...will then not even prove sufficient and will have to be increased far more...it will create new needs and at the same time create the means for their satisfaction' (*Fundamental Principles of Communism* [1847], quoted in E. Kamenka, *The Ethical Foundations of Marxism* [rev. edn, Routledge & Kegan Paul, London, 1972].

his view that the stationary state was unlikely, 'in any of the great countries of Europe, to be soon actually reached'.[26] What distinguished J.S. Mill's position from that of the classical school from Smith to Ricardo was his frank admission that he could not 'regard the stationary state of capital and wealth with the unaffected aversion so generally manifested towards it by political economists of the old school'.[27]

For one thing, he favoured what we have recently learned to call Zero Population Growth. While granting that 'there is room in the world, no doubt, and even in old countries, for a great increase of population', he confessed that he could 'see very little reason for desiring it', and not merely for Malthusian reasons. 'A population may be too crowded, though all be amply supplied with food and raiment... It is not good for man to be kept perforce at all times in the presence of his species. A world from which solitude is extirpated, is a very poor ideal'.[28]

He could find little more to be said for growth of per capita income than for growth of population. He declared himself

> not charmed with the ideal of life held out by those who think that the normal state of human beings is that of struggling to get on; that the trampling, crushing, elbowing, and treading on each other's heels, which form the existing type of social life, are the most desirable lot of human kind, or anything but the disagreeable symptoms of one of the phases of industrial progress... Those who do not accept the present very early stage of human improvement as its ultimate type, may be excused for being comparatively indifferent to the kind of economical progress which excites the congratulations of ordinary politicians; the mere increase of production and accumulation.[29]

Mill was prepared to concede that, until 'the better minds succeed in educating the others into better things', it is more desirable that the energies of mankind be employed in the struggle for riches than that they should rust and stagnate. 'While minds are coarse they require coarse stimuli; and let them have them.' He also granted the mercantilists' point that 'for the safety of national independence it is essential that a country should not fall much behind its neighbours in these things'.[30] But he could see no objective case for further economic growth in the advanced countries: 'It is only in the backward countries of the world that increased production is still an important object: in those most advanced, what is economically needed is a better distribution.'[31] And his personal preference was quite clear.

> If the earth must lose that great portion of its pleasantness which it owes to things that the unlimited increase of wealth and population would extirpate from it...I sincerely hope, for the sake of posterity, that they will be content to be stationary, long before necessity compels them to it.[32]

Mill, like Marx, was an intellectual who looked down with contempt on the crass pursuit of riches by his well-to-do contemporaries, and even perhaps on the coarse taste of the masses for more consumption, though he shared with Marx a broad and abstract sympathy for the condition of the working class. With at least half of his mind, he belonged to the minority who, throughout the nineteenth century, from Coleridge and Southey to Disraeli and Carlyle, Maurice and Kingsley, Morris and Ruskin, Thoreau and Veblen,[33] voiced their dissent from the predominant spirit of the age, protesting against the vulgar materialism and injustice of capitalist progress.*

John Stuart Mill was the last major English economist to share the interest in economic growth of the classical economists from Adam Smith. For the rest of the nineteenth century and for most of the first half of the twentieth, the economics profession turned to other problems, the theory of value and distribution, welfare economics, monetary and trade cycle theory, all these treated almost entirely on static assumptions. And while expressions of dissent from the ethos of material progress continued, hardly a line is to be found in the writings of any professional economists between 1870 and 1940 in support of economic growth as a policy objective.†

---

*Three years before the appearance of Mill's *Principles*, the young Tory radical, Disraeli, had written in *Sybil*: 'To acquire, to accumulate, to plunder each other by virtue of philosophic phrases, has been the breathless business of enfranchised England for the last twelve years, until we are startled from our voracious strife by the wail of intolerable serfage.' And a few years earlier still, Mill's friend, Carlyle, had thundered in *Chartism* against a society in which 'Cash Payment is the universal sole nexus of man to man'.

†T.W. Hutchison's detailed and comprehensive *Review of Economic Doctrines 1870–1929* (Clarendon Press, Oxford, 1953) does not contain a single reference, explicit or implicit, to economic growth as an objective of economic policy.

Hicks has attributed this change to the personal influence of J.S. Mill.

> It is John Mill...who killed the Old Growth Economics and paved the way for the Static Epoch which was to follow... It is not easy to trace the direct influence of these views of Mill's on the next generation; but that they did have a great influence, even if it was an indirect, or unconscious, influence seems to me hardly doubtful. After all, we do know that Mill's book was read very widely.[34]

No doubt, 'much must have been soaked up from Mill', but it seems more realistic to see Mill as the first, or at any rate most influential, voice to express new policy priorities.

The classical economists from Adam Smith to Ricardo had been intensely interested in economic growth because they thought it desirable and because they advocated government policies which they believed would promote it, chiefly policies of *laissez faire*, of less government interference. By the mid-nineteenth century, these policies had been substantially adopted, with spectacular success. It did not need economists to advocate material progress which was conspicuously under way. Instead, economists, apart from pursuing the scientific task of improving and perfecting the analytical work of the classics on the working of a market economy, felt it increasingly necessary to direct their attention to the evils, or at least the blemishes, of the existing system — inequality in the distribution of income and wealth, the growth of monopolies and combines, the trade cycle and unemployment.

The Static Epoch

To attempt to demonstrate how little interest the economics profession showed, over a period of some seventy or eighty years, in economic growth as a policy objective by quoting the few exceptions that prove the rule is liable to have the opposite effect of that intended. But with that warning in mind, a little should be said about the three main figures of the pre-1914 period before we turn to the inter-war years.

Marshall, in his views on the desirability and likelihood of continuing economic growth, differed only in shades of emphasis from Mill. Like Mill, he could see

> no good reason for believing that we are anywhere near a stationary state in which there will be no new important wants to be satisfied; in which there will be no more room for profitably investing present effort in providing for the future, and in which the accumulation of wealth will cease to have any reward. The

whole history of man shows that his wants expand with the growth of his wealth and knowledge... The rate of progress has sometimes been slow, and occasionally there has even been a retrograde movement; but now we are moving on at a rapid pace that grows quicker every year; and we cannot guess where it will stop.[35]

And this assessment, written for the first edition of the *Principles* in 1890, he saw no cause to alter for the eighth edition in 1920.

On the desirability of this material progress he was more judicious, less disparaging than Mill, while making it very clear that there are higher things.

The truth seems to be that as human nature is constituted, man rapidly degenerates unless he has some hard work to do, some difficulties to overcome... There is some misuse of wealth in all ranks of society; but, speaking generally, we may say that every increase in the income of the working classes adds to the fulness and nobility of human life because it is used chiefly in the supply of real wants; yet even among the artisans in England, and perhaps still more in new countries, there are signs of the growth of that unwholesome desire for wealth as a means of display which has been the chief bane of the well-to-do classes in every civilised country... So long as wealth is applied to provide for every family the necessaries of life and culture, and an abundance of the higher forms of enjoyment for collective use, so long the pursuit of wealth is a noble aim; and the pleasures which it brings are likely to increase with the growth of those higher activities which it is used to promote.[36]

A reminder in the first edition that 'poverty causes mental and moral degradation' was later dropped and replaced by a homily on how 'the world would go much better if everyone would buy fewer and simpler things, and would take trouble in selecting them for their real beauty'.[37]

The great Swedish economist, Knut Wicksell, illustrates the paradox which was to become even more apparent in the inter-war period. Neither his important contribution to the theory of capital as a factor of production, nor his path-breaking analysis of the role of investment in the trade cycle, led him into any serious analysis of the process of economic growth or discussion of economic growth as an objective of policy. When he came to discuss the accumulation of capital in his *Lectures* (1901), he advanced little beyond Mill in examining the factors which delay the secular decline in the rate of profit.[38] His expectations for the future were dominated by his neo-Malthusianism: 'The unprecedented growth of population recently witnessed in Europe, and still more in certain extra-European countries, will certainly, sooner or later — probably in the course of the present century — prepare the way for much slower progress and possibly for completely stationary conditions.'[39] Unlike Mill, he thought 'such a state would be far from desirable in an individualistic society based on private property', for the very Ricardian reason that 'the gulf between the propertied and the property-less classes would be well-nigh impassible if land, capitalized at an extremely low rate of interest, possessed almost infinite exchange value'.[40]

Just before the First World War Schumpeter published the only major non-Marxist work of the period which dealt directly with economic growth under capitalism, his *Theory of Economic Development*. Although its aim and method, as he emphasised, was 'frankly "theoretical"',[41] to analyse the process of secular economic change, it was, very consciously though not avowedly, a reply to the Marxist critique of capitalism, as well as an attack on some of the errors in static neo-classical theory. Schumpeter explicitly defined the process of development as different from 'mere growth of the economy, as shown by the growth of population and wealth',* for he saw as the essence of development the emergence of 'qualitatively new phenomena'[42] especially those changes in the way of doing things, including new processes and new products, which he called 'innovations'. Although, as an intellectual, he approved of capitalism chiefly as a dynamic civilisation, its 'cultural values and ideals', he did not despise the economic growth it had yielded and thought even the trade cycle a price worth paying. 'In a society with private property and competition, this process is the necessary complement of the continual emergence of new economic and social forms and of continually rising incomes of all social strata.'[43] Thirty years later, when he had become very pessimistic about the future of capitalism — not because 'it is breaking down under the weight of economic failure, but [because] its very success undermines the social institutions which protect it'[44] — he still insisted on the 'impressive economic and the still more impressive cultural achievement of the capitalist order'.[45] But he did not think this was enough of an argument 'for allowing the capitalist process to work on and, as it might easily be

---

*It is worth noting that this (to my knowledge the very first) use by an economist of the term economic growth in the modern sense appears in the context of the distinction between 'mere growth' and 'development'.

put, to lift poverty from the shoulders of mankind — even if mankind were...free to choose'.[46] 'As regards the economic performance, it does not follow that men are "happier" or even "better off" in the industrial society of today than they were in the medieval manor or village,'[47] In any case, 'one may care less for the efficiency of the capitalist process in producing economic and cultural values than for the kind of human beings that it turns out and then leaves to their own devices, free to make a mess of their lives'.[48] But, in 1943 as in 1911, Schumpeter stood alone in his interests and in his judgments, as an observer and as a prophet.

The Inter-War Years: Stability and Security

In 1919, surveying the turmoil and misery of war-devastated Europe, Keynes feared that the law of diminishing returns was at last reasserting itself. The Malthusian devil, chained up for a half century and out of sight, had now perhaps been loosed again.[49] 'The extraordinary occurrences of the past two years in Russia, that vast upheaval of Society...may owe more to the deep influences of expanding numbers than to Lenin or to Nicholas'.[50] These fears proved unfounded. Productive capacity, not least of food overseas, was quickly restored. Within two years, a severe post-war depression signalled what was to become the central concern of economic policy in the western countries during the inter-war years: stability and security.

As early as 1923, D.H. Robertson declared the trade cycle to be

the most difficult in theory, and the most important in practice, of the unsolved problems of business life and economic science... It is by its success or failure in coping with this problem that the present order of industry — Capitalism or Private Enterprise, or whatever you like to call it, will increasingly be judged.[51]

A year later he added: 'Public opinion has shown in recent years an increasing tendency to fasten on the insecurity hanging over the lives of the wage-earning population as the crucial problem of domestic affairs.'[52] Until the Great Depression of 1929 to 1933, external problems arising from the drastically changed international position of the British economy rivalled domestic affairs in the concerns of British governments — such problems as how 'to free trading in world markets, to stabilise currencies on the gold standard, to revive the international loan market'.[53]

Meanwhile, a period of spectacular economic growth began in

the United States. 'For nearly seven years the prosperity band-wagon rolled down Main Street.'[54] But few economists, any more than businessmen or politicians, believed that to promote growth was the business of government. President Coolidge 'honestly believed that by asserting himself as little as possible and by lifting the tax burdens of the rich he was benefiting the whole country — as perhaps he was'.[55] Economic growth was hardly ever discussed by academic economists, and then only in an abstract analytical context.[56] Until the Depression pushed all other concerns into the background, American economists tended to think of trust-busting and other forms of social control of business as the aspect of economic life 'about which present-day thought and action are more and more centering'.[57]

There is no need to quote chapter and verse for the degree to which the twin problems of stability and security became the all-consuming preoccupation of economists, as of public and politicians, from 1929 onwards, leading to the analytical breakthrough in Keynes's *General Theory* and in Britain to the two wartime Beveridge reports on *Social Security* and *Full Employment*, as in the United States through the New Deal to the *Full Employment Act* of 1945. What is worth emphasising is the effect of the Depression — with its consequences in massive unemployment, idle factories, output quotas, burning and dumping of food surpluses — in depreciating productivity and growth as desirable economic objectives. The blatant evidence all around of 'poverty in the midst of plenty' led many, at least in western countries, to a real conviction that the problem of production was solved and all that mattered now was the problem of distribution.

On a much more sophisticated plane, if not perhaps too seriously, Keynes, in his 1930 essay on 'Economic Possibilities for our Grandchildren' referred to earlier, standing back and taking a long view, was prepared to regard the Depression as 'a temporary phase of maladjustment' and to 'predict that the standard of life in progressive countries one hundred years hence will be between four and eight times as high as it is to-day'.[58]

> I draw the conclusion that, assuming no important wars and no important increase in population, the *economic problem* may be solved, or be at least within sight of solution, within a hundred years. This means that the economic problem is not — if we look into the future — *the permanent problem of the human race.*

When man arrives at his destination, 'economic bliss', he will 'for the first time since the creation...be faced with his real, his permanent problem — how to use his freedom from pressing economic cares, how to occupy the leisure which science and compound interest will have won him, to live wisely and agreeably and well'.[59]

Precursors

It was among a few voices of protest against the prevailing public pressures and government policies for stability and security at almost any price, that one finds an occasional reminder that economic growth still matters. Pointing in 1934 to the 'public policy of restrictionism' — as illustrated by the *Agricultural Adjustment Act*, 'orderly marketing', protection of railways against road transport competition and all such attempts to preserve the value of capital already invested in particular industries — as inconsistent with economic progress, Robbins disclaimed the right of economists to decide whether economic progress is desirable but thought it

> pertinent to observe that the majority of the human race are still very poor and that if, in the interests of a supposed stability, a halt is to be called in the process of raising real incomes, it is an issue which should be squarely presented to those who are most affected by it. It is all very well for the dilettante economists of wealthy universities, their tables groaning beneath a sufficiency of the good things of this world, their garages furnished with private means of transport, to say, 'Food is cheap enough. Charabancs are vulgar. The railways are admirable. We have enough of plenty. Let us safeguard security.' It is for the millions to whom a slice of bacon more or less, or a bus ride to the sea, still matter, to make a decision.[60]

In the following year, an economist who had been disturbed by the view 'practically universal in Australia and New Zealand' that a sound development policy must provide for indefinite expansion of rural population engaged in agriculture, devoted a whole book, under the title *The Clash between Progress and Security*, to 'the implications of material progress for the structure and organisation of industry as a whole'.[61] The author, A.G.B. Fisher, did not think it necessary

to consider whether progress, interpreted in the light of some
philosophical view of man and the universe, is either possible or
desirable... It is sufficient for our purpose that the objective conditions do exist upon which [material] progress depends, and that
a large proportion of the inhabitants of modern communities
desire to enjoy the material progress which these conditions make
possible.[62]

'No reputable economist has ever maintained that material progress was an end, good in itself, for the sake of which everything
else had to be sacrificed.' But in trying 'to decide how far material
progress is to be made the sole or ultimate objective of economic
policy or how far it should be sacrificed in the interests of individual security or stability [or] other ends which conflict with
material progress',[63] we should, he thought, bear in mind a
number of considerations which tell in favour of continuing
economic progress. 'If economic progress were to cease to-day,
we should find it necessary to submit to rigid and ossified social
stratification, which is rightly abhorrent to large sections of modern public opinion.'[64] People living in a capitalist society can
hardly be expected to

rest satisfied with existing living standards... The gross inequalities
of capitalist society, if they are to be justified at all, can find
justification only in the belief that sufficient plasticity and flexibility are maintained to make possible a steady if irregular
improvement in the standard of living, while at the same time
opportunities are offered from time to time to individuals to
transfer to departments of work where the level of remuneration
is higher.

Like Robbins, he thought it

worthy of note that the people who express doubts about the
value of further material progress are usually people who, even in
these depressed years, enjoy a considerable degree of comfort... It
is not easy to discuss patiently with them their complacent relega-
tion of other people to permanently depressed living standards.
The time may come when we may reasonably call a halt, satisfied
that everybody everywhere has reasonable opportunities for living
a civilised life, but that time is clearly far distant.[65]

Towards the very end of the inter-war period, the process of
economic growth began, after a lapse of eighty or so years, once
again to engage the attention of economists. One source of this

renewed interest was the paradox of Keynesian income theory: investment generated income and effective demand but had, seemingly, no effect on supply through additions to the stock of capital. It was the Swedish economist, Lundberg, who first pointed out, a few months after the publication of Keynes's *General Theory*, that it is only in 'an expanding economic system' that 'it is possible to view capital formation from its simplest and most important perspective, namely as a means of increasing the production of consumer goods' and to pose the question 'whether this growth can continue in some sort of dynamic equilibrium'.[66] The task of 'dynamising Keynes' was carried further by Harrod, in an important article published in 1939, and later by Domar.[67] As we shall see, this purely analytical work contributed after the Second World War to the increasing emphasis on economic growth as a policy objective.

The second contribution came from the work of national income statisticians, Bowley and Clark in England and Kuznets in the United States. As early as 1904, Bowley had begun the task of measuring economic growth: 'It is only by looking at figures year by year for a long period that the rate of economic progress can be estimated.'[68] Colin Clark, in his second work, *National Income and Outlay*, completed in 1936, was probably the first to think in terms of an annual 'rate of growth of real income per head of the population' and to try to estimate this magnitude statistically.[69]*

But it was in his great work, *The Conditions of Economic Progress*, written in the four years after Keynes's *General Theory* and (no doubt consciously) echoing in its title the fourth volume of his *Principles* which Marshall planned but never wrote,[70] that Colin Clark returned the economics profession to the classical concern with economic growth. Designed as

---

*The following remarkable passage from this book is worth quoting, and not merely because it is the earliest reference to 'the rate of economic growth' I have come across:

'I have stated above a positive view of the conditions dominating the long-term possibilities of an increase in productivity, because I believe the facts have destroyed the view up till now generally prevalent, i.e. that the rate of economic growth was primarily dependent upon the rate at which capital could be accumulated... Without new investment the replacement of obsolete capital...appears to give all the necessary scope for the introduction of technical and organisational improvements' (p. 272).

a comparative study of the investigations which have been made in all the principal countries into national income...oriented in such a direction as to give us as much information as possible on the matter which after all concerns us most — namely, to find the conditions under which we can hope for the greatest degree of economic progress in the future,[71]

the book presented for the first time solid quantitative evidence of the fact that 'the world...is a wretchedly poor place... Oft-repeated phrases about poverty in the midst of plenty, and the problems of production having already been solved if only we understood the problems of distribution, turn out to be the most untruthful of all modern clichés.'[72]

> The under-utilisation of productive capacity is a question of considerable importance only in the U.S.A.... For most of the world it is entirely subsidiary to the much more important fact that, with productive resources fully employed, they can produce so little. The age of plenty will still be a long while in coming.[73]

Economic growth as a policy objective needed no other support than this, but it took another decade and many other pressures on the minds of economists, politicians and the public before it began to exert a major influence on public policy in the western countries.

'Industrial Leadership'

The foregoing brief sketch of the history of ideas on economic growth as a policy objective before 1945 has drawn preponderantly on British sources, from Bacon, Hume and Adam Smith to Keynes, Robbins and Clark. This may, in one important respect, have given it an unbalanced perspective.

Britain led the way in capitalist development. Under the Tudors, Stuarts and Hanoverians, the commercial and industrial development of Britain was fostered by strong government, with the full support of economists of the mercantilist school. From the mid-eighteenth century until 1914, most British economists were convinced that economic progress demanded less government and, when the dismantlement of mercantilist restraints had been substantially accomplished, that it could be left to look after itself, basically for the reason which still convinced Marshall in 1919: 'It seems to remain almost as true now, as in former times, that the heavy hand of Government tends to slacken progress in whatever it touches.'[74] Economic growth, therefore, while generally regarded as eminently desirable, never throughout this period appeared *in Britain* as an important objective of government policy.

In the countries which were behind England in industrial development the argument that economic growth can be left to look after itself never carried complete conviction. From Alexander Hamilton, arguing in his *Report on Manufactures* of 1791 in favour of government bounties to promote 'the growth of this species of industry', to Friedrich List's rejection of the classical economists' case for free trade on the ground that the true political economy is 'that policy which each separate nation has to obey to make progress in its economical conditions',[75] the majority of non-British economists throughout the nineteenth century probably regarded national economic development as requiring positive government measures of one kind or another; and apart from the desirability of economic growth as a means of increasing the living standards and welfare of the people, most of them sympathised in varying degree with nationalist public sentiment which regarded the need to catch up with, or at least not to fall too greatly behind, Britain as a valid and important motive for economic growth as a policy objective.

It is no accident that the only context in which Marshall discussed economic development in his last book, *Industry and Trade*, written before and during the First World War and published in 1919, was that of 'industrial leadership' among the nations of the world which Britain had enjoyed for so long and seemed now in danger of losing.[76] The history of nineteenth century economic thought in Germany, Russia and Japan would almost certainly reveal much more emphasis, if only implicit, on economic growth as a policy objective. We shall see national rivalry re-emerging in the 1950s as an important motive behind policies for economic growth.

References

1 Quoted in J.B. Bury, *The Idea of Progress* (Macmillan, London, 1924), p. 52.

2 *Ibid.*, p. 128. Bury's book is still one of the best sources on the subject of this paragraph. See also J. Passmore, *The Perfectibility of Man* (Duckworth, London, 1970).

3 J.M. Keynes, *Essays in Persuasion* (Macmillan, London, 1933), p. 360.

4 Francis Bacon, *The History of the Reign of King Henry the Seventh*, quoted in E. Whittaker, *A History of Economic Ideas* (Longmans Green, New York, 1940), p. 283.

5 *The Works of Sir James Steuart* (London, 1805), vol. 1, p. 348, quoted in Whittaker, *op. cit.*, p. 293.

6 David Hume, 'Of Commerce', in *Essays and Treatises on Several Subjects,* p. 275, quoted in Whittaker, *op. cit.*, p. 295.

7 Adam Smith, *The Wealth of Nations* (first published 1776; ed. E. Cannan, University Paperbacks, London, 1961), vol. 1, p. 91.

8 *Ibid.*, p. 367.

9 *Ibid.*, p. 88.

10 Mercier de la Rivière, *L'ordre naturel et essentiel des sociétés politiques* (1767), quoted in Bury, *op. cit.*, p. 173.

11 Hla Myint, *Theories of Welfare Economics* (Longmans Green, London, 1948), p. 70.

12 Smith, *op. cit.*, p. 106.

13 Quoted in J.A. Schumpeter, *History of Economic Analysis* (Oxford University Press, New York, 1954), p. 740.

14 *The Works and Correspondence of David Ricardo* (ed. P. Sraffa, Cambridge University Press, Cambridge, 1951) vol. 1 (*Principles of Political Economy and Taxation*), p. 93.

15 J.R. Hicks, 'Growth and Anti-Growth', *Oxford Economic Papers*, November 1966, p. 260.

16 Ricardo, *op. cit.*, pp. 424–5.

17 Cf. Joan Robinson, *An Essay on Marxian Economics* (Macmillan, London, 1942), ch. 5; J.A. Schumpeter, *Capitalism, Socialism and Democracy* (Allen & Unwin, London, 1943), pp. 29 ff.; G.L.S. Tucker, 'Marx and the Theory of Increasing Misery' (mimeographed, Australian National University, 1975).

18 E. Kamenka, *The Ethical Foundations of Marxism* (rev. edn, Routledge & Kegan Paul, London, 1972), p. 155.

19 Karl Marx, *Oekonomisch-philosophische Manuskripte* (first published 1844; Marx-Engels Werke, Berlin, 1968), p. 546.

20 Karl Marx and Friedrich Engels, *Communist Manifesto* (1848), quoted in Schumpeter, *Capitalism, Socialism and Democracy*, p. 7.

21 Karl Marx, *The German Ideology*, quoted in Passmore, *op. cit.*, p. 283.

22 Karl Marx, *Kritik des Gothaer Programms* (first published 1891; Marx-Engels Werke, Berlin, 1962), vol. 19, p. 21.

23 Kamenka, *op. cit.*, pp. 156–7.

24 Schumpeter, *History of Economic Analysis*, p. 531.

25 J.S. Mill, *Principles of Political Economy* (5th edn, Parker, London, 1862), vol. 2, p. 301.

26 *Ibid.*

27 *Ibid.*, p. 322.

28 *Ibid.*, p. 325.

29 *Ibid.*, p. 323.

30 *Ibid.*

31 *Ibid.*, p. 324.

32 *Ibid.*, p. 325.

33 Cf. W. Harrison, *Conflict and Compromise: History of British Political Thought 1593–1900* (The Free Press, New York, 1965), pp. 169 ff.

34 Hicks, *op. cit.*, pp. 260, 262.

35 A. Marshall, *Principles of Economics* (9th edn, ed. C.W. Guillebaud, Macmillan, London, 1961), vol. 1, p. 223.

36 *Ibid.*, pp. 136–7.

37 *Ibid.*, p. 137.

38 K. Wicksell, *Lectures on Political Economy* (English translation, Routledge & Kegan Paul, London, 1934), vol. 1, part 3.

39 *Ibid.*, p. 214.

40 *Ibid.*

41 J.A. Schumpeter, *The Theory of Economic Development* (English translation, Harvard University Press, Cambridge, Mass., 1936), p.x.

42 *Ibid.*, p. 63.

43 *Ibid.*, p. 255.

44 Schumpeter, *Capitalism, Socialism and Democracy*, p. 61.

45 *Ibid.*, p. 129.

46 *Ibid.*

47 *Ibid.*

48 *Ibid.*

49 J.M. Keynes, *The Economic Consequences of the Peace* (Macmillan, London, 1920), p. 8.

50 *Ibid.*, pp. 12–13.

51 D.H. Robertson, 'The Stabilisation of Employment', reprinted in D.H. Robertson, *Economic Fragments* (P.S. King & Son, London, 1931), p. 130.

52 'Family Endowment', *ibid.*, p. 145.

53 E.V. Francis, *Britain's Economic Strategy* (Jonathan Cape, London, 1939), p. 10.

54 F.L. Allen, *Only Yesterday* (first published 1931; Penguin, London, 1938), vol. 1, p. 213.

55 *Ibid.*, p. 246.

56 Cf. F.H. Knight, 'Statics and Dynamics' (1930), reprinted in F.H. Knight, *The Ethics of Competition* (Harper & Row, New York, 1936).

57 J.M. Clark, *Social Control of Business* (Chicago University Press, Chicago, 1926), p. xi.

58 Keynes, *Essays in Persuasion*, pp. 364–5.

59 *Ibid.*, pp. 367–8.

60 L.C. Robbins, *The Great Depression* (Macmillan, London, 1934), pp. 143–4.

61 A.G.B. Fisher, *The Clash between Progress and Security* (Macmillan, London, 1935), pp. v, vii.

62 *Ibid.*, pp. 1–2.

63 *Ibid.*, pp. 5–6.

64 *Ibid.*, pp. 3–4.

65 *Ibid.*, p. 4.

66 E. Lundberg, *Studies in the Theory of Economic Expansion* (Stockholm Economic Studies, No. 6, P.S. King & Son, London, 1937).

67 R.F. Harrod, 'An Essay in Dynamic Theory', *Economic Journal*, 1939, reprinted in R.F. Harrod, *Economic Essays* (Macmillan, London, 1952).

68 A.L. Bowley, *Statistical Studies Relating to National Progress in Wealth and Trade since 1882: a plea for a further enquiry* (P.S. King & Son, London, 1904), p. xi.

69 Colin Clark, *National Income and Outlay* (Macmillan, London, 1938), p. 264.

70 A.C. Pigou (ed.), *Memorials of Alfred Marshall* (Macmillan, London, 1925), p. 65.

71 Colin Clark, *The Conditions of Economic Progress* (Macmillan, London, 1940), p. vii.

72 *Ibid.*, pp. 2–3.

73 *Ibid.*, pp. 3–4.

74 A. Marshall, *Industry and Trade* (3rd edn, Macmillan, London, 1920), p. 672.

75 F. List, *The National System of Political Economy* (first published 1841; Longmans, London, 1922), p. 141.

76 Marshall, *Industry and Trade*, chs 3–5.

3 The Groundswell

When the Second World War ended, there was no doubt in the minds of the great majority of economists, politicians and the general public in the west that 'the most important of [post-war economic] problems is that of providing for *continuing full employment*'.[1] In 1940 President Roosevelt had proclaimed 'freedom from want' as one of the Four Freedoms, and the Atlantic Charter of August 1941 had included 'economic advancement' for all, as well as 'improved labour standards' and 'social security', among the economic peace aims of the Anglo-American alliance.[2] The worldwide scale of the conflict and its political repercussions in Asia and Africa had begun to direct attention to problems of economic development in the less developed regions of the world.[3] But all through the war and for some years after, thinking about peacetime domestic economic policy was dominated by concern for stability and security, with full employment as the prime objective.

Full Employment — Preferably without Inflation

In Britain the war years crystallised all the grim memories of the depressed 1930s and hopes for the future in the notion of the welfare state, as expounded by the two Beveridge Reports on *Social Security* (1942) and *Full Employment in a Free Society* (1944). Pessimism about the possibility of full employment in a capitalistic democracy[4] gave way to 'wide agreement...that a high level of employment was a practicable objective of the highest priority'.[5] In the Government White Paper of 1944, all parties accepted 'as one of their primary aims and responsibilities the maintenance of a high and stable level of employment after the war'.[6] Similar proclamations of high or full employment as a government responsibility were made by governments of various political

27

complexions in Sweden, Canada, Australia, New Zealand and South Africa,[7] and a full employment pledge was incorporated in the Charter of the United Nations.[8]

Even in the United States, where Keynesian economics and the welfare state encountered much stronger conservative opposition, Congress was persuaded to pass the *Employment Act* of 1946 which imposed on the federal government responsibility for maintaining, if not full employment, at least 'high levels of employment' and set up a Council of Economic Advisers to advise the President on 'national economic policies to foster and promote free competitive enterprise, to avoid economic fluctuations, or to diminish the effects thereof, and to maintain employment, production and purchasing power'.[9]

Under the impact of the Great Depression and the failure of the New Deal to restore buoyancy to the American economy, the Keynesian analysis had in the United States been developed into the doctrine of secular stagnation associated especially with the name of Alvin Hansen. Believing that the war had merely postponed the problem, and remembering the severe post-war depression that had followed the First World War, American economists, with few exceptions, were convinced that the restoration of peace would bring back deficient aggregate demand and massive unemployment. When VE Day reduced the war to one front, the United States was warned to 'anticipate unemployment or under-employment of around five million men'.[10] Crude econometric projections, based on pre-war consumption function estimates and neglecting the huge wartime accumulation of personal savings and deferred consumer demand, predicted anywhere from five to eleven million unemployed in the first post-war spring.[11] When the Pabst Brewing Company of Milwaukee organised an essay contest on post-war employment, it was inundated by 36 000 entries (the first and second prizes going to future chairmen of the Council of Economic Advisers).[12] One of the last economic reports published by the League of Nations was on *Economic Stability in the Post-War World* (1945); one of the first of the United Nations on *National and International Measures for Full Employment* (1949).[13]

Even the prompt and successful absorption of millions of ex-servicemen and war production workers into the peacetime economy and continuance of boom conditions were slow to break down the conviction that 'our number one problem is not the nineteenth-century one of production, but the twentieth-century problem of demand'.[14] For several years after the war, every dip in economic activity and employment in the American economy was suspected, at home and abroad, of being the beginning of the long-awaited post-war depression.

> The citizens and governments of most nation states fear the occurrence of large-scale unemployment more than any other disaster that can happen in peace. No government of the future can hope to stay for long in power if it lets large-scale unemployment destroy the physical and spiritual conditions of life among the people.[15]

While full employment remained the categorical imperative of economic policy, it became increasingly apparent with every passing year that the chief threat to economic stability in the post-war economy came from excess rather than deficiency of aggregate demand. As should have been obvious, though few economists had foreseen it clearly, in a world whose productive capacity had for years been pre-empted for war and partly destroyed by it, there was no shortage of investment opportunities. Needs were urgent and the new-found determination everywhere to maintain full employment at almost any price reinforced pressures from all quarters to overspend. The editor of an American book on income stabilization, begun in 1946 but not published until 1953, described the changing focus in the United States:

> This book...was conceived in 1946 at a time when it appeared that all the instruments of policy might have to be mobilized to meet the problem of a major postwar depression. Later, when first drafts of some of the chapters became available, it seemed inconceivable that there could be a threat to stability from any cause but inflation. As later drafts came under review we moved through the mild recession of 1949 and the post-Korean inflation into [a] period of relative stability of prices, employment and the money market. At this writing...opinion is divided as to whether stability is menaced more in the immediate future by an insufficiency of demand growing out of the tapering off of the defense program or by a further burst of inflationary forces.[16]

In Britain, and in varying degrees in all the war-torn countries of western Europe, post-war shortages threatened both internal and external balance. The British Labour government came to power in 1945 'committed to planning — or re-planning — the whole economy',[17] but circumstances compelled it to give priority to the urgent twin problems of demand management, how to contain inflation at home and how to cope with a critical balance of payments problem.

During the late 1940s and early 1950s, as fears of a major depression subsided and full employment targets became more ambitious,[18] inflation was increasingly recognised as the chronic disease of a fully employed market economy, and the emphasis in policy for internal balance shifted towards some admixture of 'incomes policy' with demand management. Similarly, as western Europe recovered from the war, and the post-war 'dollar shortage' gave way during the 1950s to a dollar glut, the emphasis in policies for external balance changed for most countries (except Britain). But none of this really explains why and how economic growth came in the 1950s to rival internal and external balance for the leading place among the objectives of economic policy. There is in fact hardly a trace of interest in economic growth as a policy objective in the official or professional literature of western countries before 1950. But it is possible to detect in the five post-war years changes in the climate of opinion which foreshadowed the ascent of growth to pre-eminence. The rest of this chapter will attempt to identify the main elements in this groundswell.

Return to Scarcity

The experience of the war itself, and of post-war shortages and austerity, induced a profound, though only half-conscious, change in attitudes. The problems of the war economy had reminded a generation accustomed to apparent surpluses that resources are limited. It had also demonstrated the astonishing capacity of modern industrial economies, and especially that of the United States, to deliver the goods. As President Roosevelt put it, in his last budget message to Congress: 'The American people have learned during the war the measure of their productive capacity.'[19]

In the immediate aftermath of war, national and personal survival in many countries depended on a desperate effort to get the economy working again, to repair and reconstruct factories, railways and power plants, to resume and expand production of the most urgently needed goods and services. Even in Britain, where conditions were less critical than on the Continent or in Japan, shortages assumed crisis proportions in the severe winter of 1947.

The British government's first annual *Economic Survey* warned sternly: 'We are compelled to expand our production if we are to obtain the essential imports of food, raw materials and machinery which are vital to maintain our standard of living even at its present level'.[20] In the depressed 1930s, increases in average output per worker had been liable to add to the number of unemployed. Now, 'with surplus manpower absorbed, the economy has...been forced against the limits of scarcity'.[21]

> Before the war the word productivity was largely confined to academic discussion. Today it is common currency. In higher productivity is seen the easiest solution to our problems, and, in a state of full employment, total output of any given composition can only expand if the productivity of individual workers increases.[22]

For some years in the late 1940s and early 1950s 'productivity' became the watchword, especially but not only in the United Kingdom. Estimates published during the war had indicated a very much higher level of output per worker in American than in British (and other European) manufacturing industry.[23] If Britain had lagged behind, there seemed scope for catching up, for increases in productivity which alone, in a fully employed economy with an almost stationary labour force, could help eliminate the 'large excess of requirements over resources',[24] the fundamental cause of the inflationary gap at home and of the foreign exchange gap in the balance of payments. 'Productivity', proclaimed the United Kingdom *Economic Survey for 1949*, 'must now come to the forefront'.[25] Productivity teams were commissioned to advise British industries. National Productivity Councils were set up in various countries, and the newly established Organisation for European Economic Cooperation (OEEC, later renamed the Organisation for Economic Cooperation and Development) created a European Productivity Agency which, in 1955, began to publish a *Productivity Measurement Review*.[26]

Return to scarcity did not at once lead to advocacy of economic growth. In the early post-war years, the problem was seen in terms of 'increased output'[27] and 'raising production'.[28] The Long Term Programme which the British government submitted to the OEEC in 1948 estimated that 'over the next four years "physical" output might be increased to a third above its pre-war level'.[29] In the United States, similarly, economists initially thought in comparative-static terms of opportunities for 'a much higher level of production', of the ability of 'every country...to produce much more than it was able to before'.[30] The first annual *Economic Survey* for the United Kingdom in which the term 'rate of growth' occurs was that for 1950.[31]

'The General Problem of Poverty'[32]

The Atlantic Charter in including in 1941 'economic advancement for all' besides improved labour standards and social security among the Allies' peace aims, and the San Francisco Charter in pledging the United Nations in 1945 to the promotion of 'higher standards of living' besides full employment and conditions of economic and social progress and development,[33] expressed sentiments arising from an incipient concern about poverty in the underdeveloped regions of the world, rather than any very specific policy objective for developed countries. Even before the war, the first statistical evidence about the extent of poverty in the depressed areas of the world had stirred consciences in the west. In the war and immediate post-war years, such humanitarian concern was lent political weight by nationalist movements for colonial emancipation, by the claims of Japan's Greater Co-prosperity Sphere and by the lure of Soviet achievements and power. Increasingly from 1943 onwards, economists interested themselves in development economics, while national governments and the new international agencies devised programmes for aid to underdeveloped countries.[34] Colin Clark, in *The Economics of 1960* (1942), predicted, on the basis of the first of all the economic growth models for the post-war world, a 'capital-hungry period' and a 'great flow of capital from Europe and America to Asia'.[35]

It seems very likely, though it would not be easy to demonstrate, that this new interest in the secular problems of underdeveloped countries was, as Kuznets has suggested, in itself a source of renewed attention to economic growth in the developed countries.[36] Certainly, there was a growing awareness of problems of poverty — apart from those due to unemployment of labour and underutilisation of capital — even here. Beveridge, in 1944, had still argued that 'in Britain, by full employment we might without any other change raise our production one-eighth above the levels reached before the war' and had wondered whether 'the best use of the whole of that increased productivity [would] be to increase the free spending power of consumers'.[37] A few years later, with a very different emphasis, Arthur Lewis urged a high rate of investment for Britain on the ground that otherwise 'the British standard of living would increase only very slowly, and the prospect of being able to abolish poverty and to give everyone a reasonable standard of material enjoyment would recede into the distance'[38] and Samuelson made the same point in more dramatic terms: 'Even the richest of such nations, the United States, would have to be hundreds of times more productive than it now is to give everybody as comfortable a standard of living as is now enjoyed by our most fortunate few.'[39]

Growth Theory

The post-war interest of the economic profession in the *theory* of economic growth had initially little if anything to do with this changing climate of opinion. It began in 1946 when Harrod in England and Domar in the United States resumed the task of 'dynamising Keynes'. In the preface to his lectures, *Towards a Dynamic Economics,* Harrod explained: 'The idea which underlies these lectures is that sooner or later we shall be faced once more with the problem of stagnation.'[40] As Domar put it later, his and Harrod's work was 'concerned with unemployment and treated growth as a remedy for it rather than an end in itself. This was partly due to the spirit of the times: the lessons of the Great Depression were still fresh in our minds.'[41]

Keynes had shown that full employment in a capitalist economy requires a level of aggregate demand equal to the aggregate supply of goods and services which a given productive capacity enables the economy to produce. Harrod and Domar examined the requirements for full employment in an economy whose productive capacity is increasing over time as a result of capital accumulation. The answer which both reached, on highly simplified assumptions, was that full employment was possible only in conditions of steady growth in which the rate of growth of all the relevant variables — income, consumption, investment, capital stock, labour forces, etc. — is equal and remains constant over time. They showed that, on their assumptions, there was only one equilibrium rate of growth, determined by the propensity to save and the capital/output ratio, and that this dynamic equilibrium was inherently unstable — Joan Robinson dubbed it the Golden Age, 'thus indicating that it represents a mythical state of affairs not likely to obtain in any actual economy'.[42]

Other economists soon pointed out that these conclusions, at least in their specific form, depended on the particular assumptions of the Harrod–Domar model. Thus began the intellectual exercise of model building which has filled thousands of pages of economic journals every year ever since and constitutes one branch of the theory of economic growth. Hahn and Matthews, in their 1964 survey of some three hundred of the more important contributions to this literature, explained the rules of the game:

> A fully articulated model of growth requires to be made up of a number of building blocks. It requires to specify functions relating to the supply of labour, saving, investment, production, technical progress and the distribution of income, to name only the most important. For each of these there are numbers of possibilities that are entirely plausible and have been seriously proposed by one writer or another. Combination of them produces thousands of possible distinct models, none of which can be dismissed as unreasonable.[43]

Concurrently, and only tenuously related to this branch of the theory of economic growth, another branch was developed by economists who, in the tradition of Marx and Schumpeter, studied the process of economic growth, trying to understand 'the way economies actually grow over time', to explain 'the variety of historical growth experience'.[44] When Abramovitz surveyed the 'Economics of Growth' in a 1951 *Survey of Contemporary Economics,* he concerned himself entirely with this aspect.[45] This was also the growth theory of two influential books which belong to the post-war years, though they were not published until the early 1950s: Arthur Lewis's *The Theory of Economic Growth* which drew on a wide range of evidence from the work of economists, economic historians, anthropologists and other social scientists to throw light on the forces likely to impede or promote economic growth in the less developed countries, and W.W. Rostow's *The Process of Economic Growth* which also concerned itself with economic growth in the real world, though its object was, in the grand manner of philosophers of history, to help solve 'the problem of formulating an alternative to the Marxist system'.[46]

For the most part, all this academic work on the theory of economic growth had little to do with economic growth as a policy objective. Initially, as we have seen, the interest in economic growth arose from policy concern with stability and full employment. The later builders of growth models may be assumed to have regarded economic growth as a good thing, but the intellectual fascination of model building did not depend on any such value judgment. If there was a causal relationship, it is probably more true that in some sense the surge of academic 'interest in problems of economic growth [was] largely an aftermath of current events'[47] than that the efflorescence of growth theory promoted the rise of economic growth as a policy objective. But academic growth theory probably exerted some influence, even before 1950.

In a general way, academic growth theory accustomed economists, and through them newspapers and politicians, to thinking about the economy in terms of 'rates of economic growth'. This 'mental revolution' for which Harrod had called in 1939[48] substantially came to pass in the post-war years and coloured policy attitudes. Academic growth theory, however, also for a while exerted a more particular influence. This was the 'expansion economics' of the Korean War years, associated especially with the names of Leon Keyserling, Chairman of President Truman's Council of Economic Advisers in Washington, and of Gunnar Myrdal, Executive Secretary of the UN Economic Commission for Europe in Geneva.

'Expansion Economics'

Leon Keyserling who during the war, in his prize-winning Pabst Award essay, had called for 'a creative offensive against unemployment'[49] was appointed Acting Chairman of the Council of Economic Advisers in October 1949. A week later, in his first Monthly Report to the President, he expounded the central idea of his expansion economics:

> We need more than a slight upward trend of business and employment... Economic stability requires economic growth, and the maximum employment and production objectives of the Employment Act require an expanding economy from year to year... We believe that your announced goal of a 300 billion economy is not just a slogan; it is the central solution to the core problems of our economy.[50]

Here was the practical policy application of the Harrod–Domar proposition that 'the preservation of full employment in a capitalist economy requires a growing income'.[51] It was perhaps the first explicit official pronouncement in favour of economic growth as a policy objective in any western country. But it was a statement in favour of economic growth as a means to full employment. It was to remain the 'theme song of the Council of Economic Advisers'[52] for the next three years.

In these three years, fears of depression in the United States gave way to fears for national security in the thickening cold war atmosphere, following the detonation of the first Soviet atom bomb in August 1949 and the outbreak of the Korean War in May 1950. The President's military advisers whose demands for greatly increased defence expenditures had previously encountered objections from economic advisers welcomed Keyserling's views, since they seemed 'to justify the economic feasibility of the national security increase they considered necessary'.[53] Keyserling's expansion economics 'now became the major "nonsecret weapon" for national security'.[54] Thus, in the United States, the full employment motive for economic growth was soon reinforced by the defence motive. To Domar, in 1951, this was the dual case for economic growth: 'The present interest in growth is not accidental; it comes on the one side from a belated awareness that in our economy full employment without growth is impossible and, on the other, from the present international conflict which makes growth a condition of survival.'[55]

Another early exponent of expansion economics was the new UN Economic Commission for Europe, under its first Executive Secretary, Gunnar Myrdal, and the first Director of its Research Division, Nicholas Kaldor. In his preface to the *Economic Survey of Europe in 1949,* Myrdal wrote: 'Europe's problems can be satisfactorily solved only within the framework of an expanding economy... Only through the expansion of production...[can] the living standards of European peoples be raised from their present levels.' So far, this is not very different from the admonitions of the post-war UK *Economic Surveys.* But quite new notes are sounded in the following lines. Economic recovery in Germany and Japan is threatening a struggle for markets which may be 'extremely disruptive...under conditions of economic stagnation... If there is a sustained growth in world production and trade, these new competitive forces could be absorbed to the general advantage of other countries'. The cold war is diverting resources from the promotion of higher living standards to military expenditures. 'Another threat to economic growth lies in the failure of a number of countries to utilize their manpower resources effectively and to find ways of stabilizing employment at high levels.' 'Underemployment of labour...in certain countries not only hampers their own economic growth but also threatens the continuation of expansion...in others.'[56]

Thus, while for Domar economic growth was still a means to full employment, for Myrdal full employment had become a means to economic growth. The growth theme was further developed in the *Survey*. It deplored a 'certain tendency in Western Europe to regard present economic programs as a non-recurrent and exceptional effort, rather than as an initial and integral part of a continued economic growth over a longer period'. It contrasted this with 'other parts of the world' where 'rapid economic progress is expected. In the Soviet Union, for example, the aim is to treble industrial output within about twenty years'.[57] A chapter on 'Problems of Sustained Economic Growth' announced confidently that the

> general slowing-down of economic progress which Europe experienced during the inter-war period need not be repeated...given appropriate policies, the potentialities exist for a large and sustained increase in production... A basic assumption underlying the perspective of a more rapid growth in the future is that it will be a steady and cumulative development.[58]

In 1949, such advocacy of economic growth, for higher living standards rather than merely for full employment, was still very rare, perhaps unique. But growth was in the air. Two years later, the English socialist writer, John Strachey, happily contrasted the stagnation of the 1930s with the

> extreme stimulation now... Not that it has been wrong...thus to drive the economy to the very limit. It was only by doing so that the all-important increase in production has been secured. The problems and difficulties...have been the problems and difficulties of growth, instead of the incomparably more morbid symptoms of stagnation and decay.

Two tasks confront the west. 'Peace can be preserved only if the Russian leaders find that the West is both completely firm and completely unaggressive.' The second task is to make its economic system work. 'That, I repeat, means turning our marvellous productive resources on to the task of steadily, and to an indefinite extent, raising the standard of life of the whole population of the world.'[59]

These early affirmations of faith in economic growth were gradually to attain wide acceptance during the 1950s.

References

1 P. Samuelson, in S.E. Harris (ed.), *Postwar Economic Problems* (McGraw Hill, New York, 1943), p. 27.

2 W.L. Neumann, *Making the Peace 1941–1945* (Foundation for Foreign Affairs, Washington, 1950), p. 11.

3 Cf. H.W. Arndt, 'Development Economics before 1945', in J.N. Bhagwati and R.S. Eckaus (eds), *Development and Planning: Essays in Honour of Paul Rosenstein-Rodan* (Allen & Unwin, London, 1972).

4 J.M. Keynes, in *New Republic*, 20 July 1940, quoted in T.W. Hutchison, *Economics and Economic Policy in Britain 1946–1966* (Allen & Unwin, London, 1968), p. 25.

5 Hutchison, *op. cit.*, p. 25.

6 *Employment Policy*, Cmd 6527, HMSO, London, May 1944, p. 1.

7 R. Lekachman, *The Age of Keynes* (Allen Lane, London, 1966), p. 150.

8 Cf. *National and International Measures for Full Employment* (Report by a Group of Experts, United Nations, New York, 1949), p. 5.

9 Lekachman, *op. cit.*, p. 147.

10 P. Samuelson, in *New Republic*, 11 September 1944, quoted in Lekachman, *op. cit.*, p. 136.

11 Lekachman, *op. cit.*, p. 138.

12 *Ibid.*, p. 133.

13 *National and International Measures for Full Employment, op. cit.*

14 S.E. Harris (ed.), *Economic Reconstruction* (McGraw Hill, New York, 1946), p. 12.

15 Oliver Franks, *Central Planning in War and Peace* (Harvard University Press, Cambridge, Mass., 1947), p. 21.

16 M.F. Millikan (ed.), *Income Stabilization for a Developing Democracy* (Yale University Press, New Haven, 1953), p. v.

17 J.C.R. Dow, *The Management of the British Economy 1945–60* (Cambridge University Press, Cambridge, 1964), p. 11.

18 Hutchison, *op. cit.*, pp. 25 ff.

19 Quoted in R.G.D. Allen, 'Post-War Economic Policy in the U.S.', *Economic Journal*, April 1945, p. 30.

20 *Economic Survey for 1947*, Cmd 7046, HMSO, London, 1947, p. 3.

21 T. Wilson, *Planning and Growth* (Macmillan, London, 1965), p. 66.

22 N.H. Leyland, in G.D.N. Worswick and P.H. Ady, *The British Economy 1945–1950* (Clarendon Press, Oxford, 1952), p. 381.

23 L. Rostas, *Comparative Productivity in British and American Industry* (National Institute of Social and Economic Research, London, 1948).

24 *Economic Survey for 1947*, p. 7.

25 *Economic Survey for 1949*, Cmd 7647, HMSO, London, p. 42.

26 (OECD, Paris), first issue, May 1955.

27 *Economic Survey for 1947*, p. 30.

28 *Economic Survey for 1949*, p. 42.

29 Dow, *op. cit.*, p. 31.

30 Mordecai Ezekiel, in Harris (ed.), *Economic Reconstruction*, p. 35.

31 *Economic Survey for 1950*, Cmd 7915, HMSO, London, p. 4.

32 D.G. Champernowne, in *Bulletin*, Oxford Institute of Statistics, 1947, p. 71.

33 *National and International Measures for Full Employment*, p. 5.

34 Arndt, *op. cit.*

35 Colin Clark, *The Economics of 1960* (Macmillan, London, 1942), pp. 110, 114.

36 S. Kuznets, in R. Lekachman (ed.), *National Policy for Economic Welfare at Home and Abroad* (Russell & Russell, New York, 1961), p. 13.

37 W. Beveridge, *Full Employment in a Free Society* (Allen & Unwin, London, 1944), p. 186.

38 W. Arthur Lewis, *The Principles of Economic Planning* (Dobson, London, 1949), p. 53.

39 P. Samuelson, *Economics* (1st edn, McGraw Hill, New York, 1948), p. 16.

40 R.F. Harrod, *Towards a Dynamic Economics* (Macmillan, London, 1949), p.v.

41 E.D. Domar, *Essays in the Theory of Economic Growth* (Oxford University Press, New York, 1957), p. 5.

42 Quoted in F.H. Hahn and R.C.O. Matthews, 'The Theory of Economic Growth: A Survey', *Economic Journal*, December 1964, reprinted in *Surveys of Economic Theory* (American Economic Association and Royal Economic Society, New York, 1967), vol. 2, p. 3.

43 Hahn and Matthews, *op. cit.*, p. 2.

44 *Ibid.*, p. 1.

45 B. Haley (ed.), *A Survey of Contemporary Economics* (Irwin, Homewood, Ill., 1952), vol. 2.

46 W.W. Rostow, *The Process of Economic Growth* (Clarendon Press, Oxford, 1953), p. 9.

47 S. Kuznets, in Haley, *op. cit.*, p. 180.

48 R.F. Harrod, 'An Essay in Dynamic Theory', *Economic Journal*, 1939, reprinted in R.F. Harrod, *Economic Essays* (Macmillan, London, 1952), p. 256.

49 E.S. Flash, *Economic Advice and Presidential Leadership* (Columbia University Press, New York, 1965), p. 22.

50 *Ibid.*, p. 28.

51 Domar, *op. cit.*, p. 71.

52 Arthur Smithies, 'Problems of Stabilization', *American Economic Association Proceedings*, May 1951, p. 186.

53 Flash, *op. cit.*, p. 38.

54 *Ibid.*, p. 59.

55 Domar, *op. cit.*, p. 18.

56 United Nations Economic Commission for Europe, *Economic Survey of Europe in 1949* (Geneva, 1950), pp. iii–iv.

57 *Ibid.*, p. 198.

58 *Ibid.*, pp. 219–20.

59 John Strachey, *Labour's Task* (Fabian Tract No. 290, London, October 1951), pp. 4, 8, 22.

4 The Ascent

At the beginning of the 1950s, as we saw in the last chapter, references to economic growth as a policy objective were still extremely rare. A few years later, in 1957, Domar, in his preface to a volume of collected essays, was able to say that 'in recent times, economic growth and development have become the fashion of the day'.[1] Domar, admittedly, had mainly in mind the current interest in growth theory and in the problems of less developed countries. But the statement was beginning to be no less true with reference to economic growth as a policy objective in the developed countries. The year before, the British government in a White Paper had declared itself 'pledged to foster conditions in which the nation can, if it so wills, realise its full potentialities for growth in terms of production and living standards'[2] and in the United States Nelson and Laurence Rockefeller had commissioned a panel of eminent citizens to prepare a report on *The Challenge of the Future* which, when it was published in 1958, turned out to be all about 'The Key Importance of Growth to Achieve National Goals'.[3] By the end of the decade, economic growth had, as one commentator has put it, been 'thrust to the top as *apparently* the supreme, overriding objective of policy'.[4] How did this happen?

One set of answers to this question was given in the 1952 United Nations *Economic Survey of Europe since the War*: 'All Governments aimed at increasing industrial and agricultural output because this was the only means to restore the balances of payments, or because of claims for higher living standards, or simply to keep in step with other countries.'[5] In the following year, Kuznets supplied another set: first, 'concern over possible secular stagnation in the industrially developed nations', then 'interest in secular prospects and problems of underdeveloped countries', and

41

thirdly, 'claims [to] greater efficiency in handling long-term economic problems [made by] the authoritarian state of the Soviet type'.[6] We shall see that all these factors played a part, and yet others need to be added to the list. But some were more important than others, at different times and different places.

Higher Living Standards

It will be well to begin with one which is so obvious that it is liable to be overlooked. By 1952 or 1953, most countries had overcome the immediate economic consequences of the Second World War, some of the worst-hit like Germany and Japan were staging a remarkable recovery, fears of a major post-war depression were receding, and the Korean War commodity boom had given way to what looked like a reasonable degree of price stability. All in all, less preoccupied and hemmed in by pressing short-term economic problems, it seemed possible to look forward more optimistically to — what?

'We should think', wrote Harrod in 1952, 'in terms of raising the real standard of living by [capital formation] and other means by 50 or 100 per cent in a generation.'[7] Two years later a Conservative Chancellor of the Exchequer took up the same theme: 'Why should we not aim to double the standard of living in the next twenty years?'[8] When Samuelson added a chapter on economic growth in the third (1955) edition of his great textbook, he prefaced the chapter by a quotation from a book on Ireland:

I believe in materialism. I believe in all the proceeds of a healthy materialism — good cooking, dry houses, dry feet, sewers, drain pipes, hot water, baths, electric lights, automobiles, good roads, bright streets, long vacations away from the village pump, new ideas, fast horses, swift conversation, theatres, operas, orchestras, bands — I believe in them all for everybody. The man who dies without knowing these things may be as exquisite as a saint, and as rich as a poet; but it is in spite of, not because of, his deprivation.[9]

There was a sense in which economic growth for higher living standards remained, to western materialists in Francis Hackett's wide interpretation, as the residual objective of economic policy when all other, more immediate, problems had been, or seemed momentarily to have been, stripped of their urgency. As Peter Wiles argued in 1956, tongue only half in cheek:

Growth is obviously the 'best' thing that can happen in economics — better than Free Trade or the attainment of the optimum allocation of resources between competing ends or even full employment. This can be very simply shown: the prime end of economic man is material plenty, he wants to have as much of everything as possible. But in order that this state of affairs should be achieved the economy must grow, i.e. production per head must be increased. Growth is then, by definition, the *sine qua non* for the attainment of the supreme end, and therefore itself supreme.[10]

Stigler, too, about the same time committed himself to a tautology which virtually made economic growth the objective of rational economic activity *by definition*: 'The Russians share the goals of maximum output and rapid economic growth. Indeed, every society that is purposive and non-traditional seeks to do efficiently whatever it seeks to do.'[11]

But this role of economic growth as residual legatee among economic policy objectives can hardly, by itself, explain the tremendous emphasis that came to be placed on it during the 1950s. Other factors contributed. For one thing, more rapid economic growth came to be regarded as a prophylactic or remedy for all the major current ailments of western economies — balance of payments difficulties and especially dollar shortage, underemployment, and inflation whether due to excess demand or competing income claims. While these arguments for economic growth were perhaps in part rationalisations, this was certainly not true of the consideration which, rationally or irrationally, came for some time to carry as much weight as all others combined: ideological and international rivalry in the 'growth' arena.

Growth for External Balance

In the post-war years, increased production was urgently needed throughout western Europe because of the elementary problem of 'a large excess of requirements over resources',[12] the gap which showed itself in domestic inflation or balance of payments deficit or both at once. Hence the emphasis on increased productivity for, as we saw, 'in a state of full employment, total output of any given composition can only expand if the productivity of individual workers increases'.[13] During the period of the Marshall Plan when United States aid temporarily helped to close the gap, a rapid increase in production in the recipient countries could be regarded as necessary 'to dispense with United States aid by the end of the period'.[14] But the dollar shortage did not disappear as quickly as had been hoped.

At first there was a tendency to see the cause of the problem in the 'grave competitive disadvantage in comparison with the U.S.' from which Europe was believed to be suffering[15] and the remedy in efforts to improve productivity 'and thereby to increase the competitive ability of European producers'.[16] When critics suggested that an absolute all-round cost disadvantage pointed to a change in exchange rates as a corrective, attempts to explain the dollar shortage turned to a more sophisticated argument. The thesis that the main explanation of the dollar shortage was a secular superiority of the United States in its rate of technical progress and growth of productivity, first put forward in 1952 by Dr T. Balogh and more systematically by Professor J. H. Williams at Harvard, was examined by Professor Hicks in his Oxford Inaugural Lecture on 'The Long-Run Dollar Problem'[17] — in which he showed that it could provide an explanation of chronic dollar shortage only on special assumptions — and became the subject of a prolonged academic debate.[18] Meanwhile, however, it gave rise to the first explicit advocacy of efforts to attain a higher rate of economic growth in Britain.

This argument for faster growth was bound to lose weight as dollar shortage gave way to dollar glut towards the end of the decade. Before this happened, however, the emphasis in British discussion of the relations between growth and the balance of payments had already changed. Official statements were still dominated by concern lest excessively rapid expansion endanger external and internal balance. The main economic objective, according to the *Economic Survey for 1953,* must continue to be the maintenance of an adequate and stable external balance and inflation must continue to be held in check.[19] The outstanding problem was still the balance of payments, said the *Economic Survey for 1954*, 'and the needs of the balance of payments must continue to govern the pace of internal expansion'.[20] This pronouncement was challenged by P.D. Henderson who questioned whether growth and external balance were in conflict and, if they were, whether this was 'a reason for slowing down the growth of the economy. The aim of economic policy should be to promote a high rate of economic growth, and to find some means of remaining solvent which is consistent with this'.[21] Henderson's statement provoked a wide-ranging debate in which a galaxy of British economic talent participated and which revealed wide divergence on both ends and means.[22] We shall have occasion in later chapters to revert to it. For the moment we need merely note that by the mid-1950s economic growth had graduated, in the minds of some economists, from being an instrument for external balance to the status of an economic objective too important to be constrained by balance of payments considerations.

Growth for Internal Balance

Until near the end of the decade, the case for growth as a means to full employment which had been relatively prominent in the post-war years found little expression. In Britain, and in Europe generally, unemployment had ceased to be a major problem. The trouble was excess, not insufficiency, of demand. Even in the United States where unemployment percentages remained significantly higher, official and public interest during most of the eight years of Republican administration under President Eisenhower switched to other issues — 'balanced budgets, debt and tax reductions, fiscal and monetary checks on inflation'.[23] Samuelson was not surprised that 'people should have begun to be a little bored with the continuous discussion of employment policy'[24] and Stigler asked whether anyone believed 'that unemployment of resources in recent years has been grievously large'.[25] Concern about the sluggishness of the American economy revived at the end of the decade, and with it advocacy of growth for full employment; but this phase is more conveniently treated in the next chapter.

All through the 1950s, it was inflation that appeared as the chief threat to internal balance in all the western countries. It is not surprising therefore that there was increasing discussion of the relations between inflation and growth. But it would be difficult to demonstrate that the emergence of economic growth as a policy objective owed much to claims for the merits of economic growth as a counter to inflation. Such claims were made. Just as it had seemed obvious after the war that 'greater production is the key to the excess demand problem',[26] so it was tempting to argue that faster growth of aggregate supply, or at any rate of productivity, was the answer to the problem of aggregate excess demand; while those who diagnosed the problem as primarily due to cost–push could argue that 'investment must be increased to accelerate the rise in productivity (and thus in the ability to satisfy wage demands)'.[27] In the technical context of fiscal and monetary policies for internal balance, all such arguments came up against the suspicion that the drive for faster growth through higher investment was itself one of the contributing causes of inflation, and in any case the discussion soon shifted to the converse question whether inflation was not a price worth paying for higher growth.[28] But in a broader context, the idea that economic growth could alleviate chronic problems of 'excess demand' or 'excess income claims' of western societies certainly played a major part in its elevation to supremacy among economic objectives.

Defusing the Class Struggle

In the fully employed British economy of the 1950s it was perhaps possible to 'imagine a society in which the problem of production might reasonably be treated as secondary' and to believe that 'these conditions are partially fulfilled in the United States', but it was apparent that they were not fulfilled in Britain, what with claims for higher personal consumption, social and productive investment, a stronger balance of payments, relief of hardship and distress at home and assistance to less developed countries abroad — all competing for limited resources. 'Improved living standards, or any other economic claims, can now be met only by higher production per head; and questions of growth and efficiency move into the forefront of matters to be attended to.'[29] In the United States, the competition among claims on resources seemed no less oppressive: 'The critical need for economic growth is found in the tasks placed upon the nation, both foreign and domestic. At no time has any free nation been faced with a greater call upon its resources.'[30]

The most insistent new claims on resources in the United States were for government expenditure on defence, provoked by the cold war, and on social overhead capital, provoked by increased awareness of the contrast, pilloried by Galbraith, between 'private affluence and public squalor'.[31] The inference was clear: 'A high rate of economic growth is essential if these public responsibilities are to be discharged without limiting the advances in living standards effected through individual efforts.'[32] 'Since in a democratic country it is difficult to increase very substantially the government's slice of the pie at the expense of the private sector, it becomes expedient to obtain a larger pie so that both sectors can increase their consumption together.'[33]

If economic growth was an answer to the problem of competing claims on resources between the private and the public sector, could it not also help resolve the social conflicts arising from the competing claims of capital and labour, rich and poor? As early as December 1950, Arthur Smithies had insisted that full employment without inflation was not enough:

> I sincerely doubt whether the struggle for redistribution can be held in check except in the context of a growing economy. Labor in particular will insist on a steady increase in its material well-being and unless total national output is increasing, the full force of this insistence will be felt in pressure for redistribution of incomes.[34]

By the end of the decade the same argument was put a little differently.

> A further reason why growth has come to receive more attention has been wider recognition of the fact that redistribution of income can at best do only a little to advance the standard of living of the bulk of the people... In modern Britain further redistribution has little to offer... If in 1962 all personal incomes from rent, interest and dividends had been somehow confiscated and handed over to the employed, without any consequential fall in output, wages and salaries would have gone up by only about 15 per cent; in fact, average real income from employment has risen by nearly a quarter in the 1950s.[35]

It was suggested that the German trade unions, whether from weakness or from wisdom, had come to realise that workers had much more to gain from growth than from redistribution. 'The fact stands out that in Germany, France and Japan, the improvement in workers' earnings and social benefits was at a rate two or three times as high [as in Britain] — despite a worsening of the distribution of income.'[36]

Galbraith summed up the argument (without associating himself with it) in 1957:

> In the advanced country...increased production is an alternative to redistribution. And...it has been the great solvent of the tensions associated with inequality... How much better to concentrate on increasing output, a programme on which both rich and poor can agree, since it benefits both... In this case the facts are inescapable. It is the increase in output in recent decades, not the redistribution of income, which has brought the great material increase, the well-being of the average man... As a result, the goal of an expanding economy has also become deeply embedded in the conventional wisdom of the American left... The oldest and most agitated of social issues, if not resolved, is at least largely in abeyance.[37]

The Soviet Challenge

In July 1953, the American quarterly, *Foreign Affairs,* published an article with the provocative title, 'The Soviet Economy Outpaces the West'.[38] The author, a young English economist, P.D. Wiles, argued

> that by whatever other criteria economies may be judged, Communism is at any rate beating 'capitalism', whether in the form of laisser faire or of the welfare state, in its rate of growth. And in a long cold war the rate of growth is the most important thing, for in the end the country that grows most becomes biggest, and every economic advantage belongs to it, be it military power, dominance in world markets or even a high standard of living.[39]

Communism will not mellow.

> Hitherto the Kremlin has become steadily more aggressive and unpleasant as its economic power has increased. It is the purest wishful thinking to suppose that, like liberalism or Socialism, Communism will kill itself by its own success... For the aims of Communism are boundless: a new man or a new earth — the whole earth.[40]

'The solution for the problem raised here lies without doubt in the economic field. We must raise our production, and keep the gap between us and them as great as it is now. Otherwise time is on their side.'[41]

The thesis was brilliantly argued and it struck a responsive chord in the United States.[42] Wiles's statistics suggesting that 'Soviet economic development betters all recorded data for the West'[43] were promptly challenged,[44] but as more official Soviet statistics became available during the Khrushchev 'thaw' they tended to confirm the impression of higher rates of growth, certainly in industrial production and certainly higher than in the United States or Britain.[45] When Khrushchev, in his speech to the Twentieth Party Congress in 1956, boasted that 'the great advantages of the socialist economic system, the high rate of development of social production, enable us to carry out in an historically very brief period the main task of the U.S.S.R. — to catch up and surpass the most developed capitalist countries in per capita output',[46] the Soviet challenge gave rise to mounting concern in the United States. It reached a stage bordering on 'hysterical anxiety'[47] when the Soviet Union in the following year beat the United States in the space race by launching its first Sputnik. 'It is

difficult to overestimate the symbolic importance of the sputnik...
One of its consequences was a public demand for vastly enlarged
American support of space technology. Inevitably, the Soviet scientific and technological accomplishments were connected with
another Soviet triumph, an exceptionally high growth rate.'[48] The
Joint Economic Committee of Congress commissioned two
studies, one in 1955 on *Trends in Economic Growth: A Comparison
of the Western Powers and the Soviet Bloc,* the other in 1957 on
Soviet Economic Growth: A Comparison with the United States.[49]
These were followed in 1959 by public hearings of the Subcommittee on Economic Statistics on 'Comparisons of the United
States and Soviet Economies' which resulted in the publication of
three volumes of expert testimony on the subject.[50]

Two quotations from well-known American economists will
illustrate the intellectual atmosphere of the time. Fellner, in a
paper on 'Rapid Growth as an Objective of Economic Policy',
delivered at the 1959 annual meeting of the American Economic
Association, thought it doubtful whether in a peaceful world there
is a case for government action to make the community save at a
higher rate than it wishes. But this is not a peaceful world. 'A vital
Western interest attaches to growth rates such as will prevent a
gradual rise to economic supremacy of the Communist bloc.'[51]
Early in 1959 two Princeton economists, Baumol and Knorr,

> became keenly interested in the growing public discussion of the
> growth performance of the American economy in the 1950s and
> its ability to sustain American security over the longer run in view
> of the persistently higher rates of economic growth in the Soviet
> Bloc... We believe that these differences [in the rate of economic
> growth] do matter and that they may threaten the ability of the
> United States to survive in a hostile world.[52]

As we shall see in the next chapter, national security was one of
the concerns — full employment being the other — which made
growth a major issue in the 1960 presidential elections.

Towards League Tables

Outside the United States, concern about the Soviet challenge
never reached the same pitch. In Britain, too, it could be said in
1956 that 'the apostles of growth have now transferred their
attention to a different quarter of the globe... The talk is now all
about the menace of Soviet industrial success'.[53] And even an
economist relatively unsympathetic to that kind of argument was

prepared to concede that 'the case for significantly increasing...the British rate of growth must rest on considerations other than "welfare" in the sense of higher consumption. In fact the strongest arguments for fearing Soviet growth are political and strategic'.[54] But generally the Soviet challenge was felt to be for the United States to accept or decline, neither Britain nor any of the other countries of western Europe being in the same league. 'Everyone except the Blimps now realizes that we cannot group ourselves with the super-powers such as the United States and Russia.'[55] But this did not mean that international comparisons of growth performance were pointless.

> Our relative power in the world is declining; what we must do is to prevent it from declining too quickly. It will not be easy to hold on to our rightful place at the top of the Second Division. It will be impossible, if the economic resources of countries such as France and Germany pull ahead of those we can command, as they may well do in the next few years.[56]

Not only advocates of growth used such arguments. Even those opposed to giving growth high priority found it politic to present their case in such terms:

> It is questionable whether Britain might not be better advised to accept and adjust to a gradual surrender of her place as a leading industrial nation, either by a planned withdrawal from the competitive struggle or by a planned transfer of productive resources (labour and capital) to other countries where the prospects of growth are better, than to attempt to retain her present relative position among the industrial nations by rapid expansion of her productive capacity.[57]

International rivalry, whether from considerations of national power or national self-esteem, has as old a history as any other motive for economic growth.[58] Sensible men may say: 'There is no point in being vain about these matters.'[59] It is precisely such matters that people in the mass are vain about. In the 1950s momentous political importance came increasingly to be attached to international comparisons of growth rates.

One reason, or at any rate a necessary precondition, was that reasonably regular and reliable statistics of GNP were only now beginning to become available.[60] In the early 1950s the OEEC and UN Economic Commission for Europe were still making comparisons of economic performance among member countries in terms of indexes of industrial and agricultural production. The OEEC published its first volume of national accounts statistics on a uniform basis for all member countries in 1954 and the second in 1957.[61] The first UN *Economic Survey of Europe* to present growth rates of real GDP, based on the OECD statistics, was that for 1957.[62]

The motive, however, which led these new statistics to be particularly eagerly, not to say morbidly, studied in Britain and the United States was that they seemed to show both countries falling behind, not merely the Soviet Union, but also the burgeoning economies of the European Economic Community and Japan. 'Since other European countries had inevitably been slower than Britain in recovering immediately after the war, it was only as their recovery advanced in the middle fifties that invidious questions of comparative growth-rates began to emerge.'[63] In the United States, too, one was 'tempted to argue...that the high rates of growth in Europe and Japan in recent years have been due in large part to attempts to "catch up"'.[64] But as the closing of the decade saw no slowing down in the momentum of the fast-growing countries or narrowing of the gap in growth rates, it came to seem necessary to look more carefully into the reasons 'why growth rates differ'.[65] This became an important academic preoccupation in the early 1960s.

References

1 E.D. Domar, *Essays in the Theory of Economic Growth* (Oxford University Press, New York, 1957), p. 5.

2 *The Economic Implications of Full Employment*, Cmd 9725, HMSO, London, March 1956, p. 12.

3 *Prospect for America* (The Rockefeller Panel Reports, Doubleday, New York, 1961), p. 320.

4 T.W. Hutchison, *Economics and Economic Policy in Britain 1946–1966* (Allen & Unwin, London, 1968), p. 207.

5 United Nations Economic Commission for Europe, *Economic Survey of Europe since the War* (Geneva, 1953), p. 9.

6 S. Kuznets, in R. Lekachman (ed.), *National Policy for Economic Welfare at Home and Abroad* (Russell & Russell, New York, 1961), pp. 12–13.

7 R.F. Harrod, 'Comment', in 'Monetary Policy: A Symposium', *Bulletin*, Oxford Institute of Statistics, April–May 1952, p. 170.

8 R.A. Butler, quoted in J.C.R. Dow, *The Management of the British Economy 1945–1960* (Cambridge University Press, Cambridge, 1964), p. 77.

9 P. Samuelson, *Economics* (3rd edn, McGraw Hill, New York, 1955), p. 703.

10· P. Wiles, 'Growth versus Choice', *Economic Journal*, June 1956, p. 244.

11 G.J. Stigler, 'The Goals of Economic Policy', *Journal of Business*, July 1958, reprinted in M.C. Grossman et al. (eds), *Readings in Current Economics* (rev. edn, Irwin, Homewood, Ill., 1961), p. 14.

12 *Economic Survey for 1947*, Cmd 7046, HMSO, London, 1947, p. 7.

13 See ch. 3, p. 31.

14 *A Decade of Co-operation: Achievements and Perspectives* (Ninth Annual Report) (OEEC, Paris, April 1958), p. 31.

15 T. Balogh, 'Monetary Restriction and Economic Progress', *Bulletin*, Oxford Institute of Statistics, June 1952, p. 249.

16 *Twelfth Annual Economic Review* (OEEC, Paris, September 1961), p. 12.

17 J.R. Hicks, 'The Long-Run Dollar Problem', *Oxford Economic Papers*, June 1953, reprinted in J.R. Hicks, *Essays in World Economics* (Clarendon Press, Oxford, 1959), pp. 66 ff.

18 See Hutchison, *op. cit.*, p. 97*n*.

19 *Economic Survey for 1953*, Cmd 8800, HMSO, London, 1953, p. 51.

20 *Economic Survey for 1954*, Cmd 9108, HMSO, London, 1954, p. 37.

21 P.D. Henderson, 'Retrospect and Prospect: The Economic Survey, 1954', *Bulletin*, Oxford Institute of Statistics, May–June 1954, p. 164.

22 'Growth and the Balance of Payments: A Symposium', *Bulletin*, Oxford Institute of Statistics, February 1955.

23 E.S. Flash, *Economic Advice and Presidential Leadership* (Columbia University Press, New York, 1965), pp. 100–1.

24 P. Samuelson, 'Full Employment versus Progress and other Goals', in M.F. Millikan (ed.), *Income Stabilization for a Developing Democracy* (Yale University Press, New Haven, 1953), p. 548.

25 Stigler, *op. cit.*, p. 16.

26 F.A. Burchardt and G.D.N. Worswick, 'Britain in Transition', *Bulletin*, Oxford Institute of Statistics, March–April 1947, p. 71.

27 T. Balogh, 'Productivity and Inflation', *Oxford Economic Papers*, June 1958, p. 240.

28 Cf. T. Wilson, 'Inflation and Growth', *Three Banks Review*, September 1961, reprinted in T. Wilson, *Planning and Growth* (Macmillan, London, 1965).

29 C.A.R. Crosland, *The Future of Socialism* (Jonathan Cape, London, 1956), pp. 375–6.

30 Joint Economic Committee on Employment, Growth and Price Levels (Douglas Committee), *Report* (US Congress, Washington, 1960), p. 11.

31 J.K. Galbraith, *The Affluent Society* (Hamish Hamilton, London, 1958; Penguin, London, 1962).

32 Douglas Committee, *op. cit.*, p. 12.

33 K. Knorr and W.J. Baumol (eds), *What Price Economic Growth?* (Prentice-Hall, Englewood Cliffs, N.J., 1961), p. 142.

34 A. Smithies, 'Problems of Stabilisation', *AEA Proceedings*, 1951, p. 186; see also W.A. Lewis, *The Theory of Economic Growth* (Allen & Unwin, London, 1955), p. 423.

35 Wilson, *op. cit.*, p. 66.

36 T. Balogh, in *New Statesman*, 14 April 1956, quoted in Hutchison, *op. cit.*, p. 67n.

37 Galbraith, *The Affluent Society*, pp. 86–7.

38 P.D. Wiles, 'The Soviet Economy Outpaces the West', *Foreign Affairs*, July 1953.

39 *Ibid.*, p. 566.

40 *Ibid.*, p. 578.

41 *Ibid.*, p. 580.

42 Cf., e.g., J.S. Davis, 'Economic Potentials of the United States', in Lekachman, *op. cit.*, p. 106.

43 Wiles, 'The Soviet Economy Outpaces the West', p. 570.

44 Cf. Colin Clark, 'The Soviet Crisis', *Encounter*, August 1955; P.D. Wiles, 'Le Trahison du Clark', *ibid.*, November 1955; Colin Clark, 'Statistical Wiles', *ibid.*, December 1955.

45 Cf. J.P. Hardt et al., *The Cold War Economic Gap* (Praeger, New York, 1961), p. 3.

46 Quoted W.W. Heller (ed.), *Perspectives on Economic Growth* (Random House, New York, 1968), p. 130.

47 R. Lekachman, *The Age of Keynes* (Allen Lane, London, 1966), p. 161.

48 *Ibid.*, p. 160. Another incidental consequence was that it improved the market for Galbraith's *Affluent Society*: 'In the autumn of that year [1957], the Soviets, as a result of much more purposeful use of a much less productive economy, surged ahead of us in the exploration of space. The questioning and anxiety which followed the first Sputnik made me certain that I would be heard. The book came out in the following spring.' (Penguin edn, p. 10).

49 For full bibliography, see Hardt, *op. cit.*, pp. 85 ff.

50 *Ibid.*

51 *AEA Proceedings*, May 1960, p. 99.

52 Knorr and Baumol, *op. cit.*, pp. v, 142; see also Isaac Deutscher, *The Great Contest* (Oxford University Press, London, 1960).

53 Crosland, *op. cit.*, p. 381.

54 *Ibid.*, p. 383.

55 Alan Day, in *Observer*, 15 November 1959, quoted in Hutchison, *op. cit.*, p. 125.

56 *Ibid.*

57 H.G. Johnson, 'Economic Expansion and the Balance of Payments', *Bulletin*, Oxford Institute of Statistics, February 1955, p. 9.

58 Cf. Hume, Mill, Marshall, quoted in ch. 2, pp. 6, 11–13, 15, 22–3.

59 Crosland, *op. cit.*, p. 383.

60 Hutchison, *op. cit.*, p. 125.

61 *Statistics of National Product and Expenditure — 1938, 1947 to 1952* (OECD, Paris, 1954), and *Statistics of National Product and Expenditure No. 2 — 1938 and 1947 to 1955* (OECD, Paris, 1957).

62 United Nations Economic Commission for Europe, *Economic Survey of Europe in 1957* (Geneva, 1958), ch. 2, p. 3.

63 Hutchison, *op. cit.*, pp. 125–6.

64 S. Kuznets, 'Patterns of US Economic Growth', in E.O. Edwards (ed.), *The Nation's Economic Objectives* (Chicago University Press, Chicago 1964), p. 32.

65 Edward F. Denison, *Why Growth Rates Differ* (Brookings Institution, Washington, D.C., 1967).

5 The Crest

The process described in the preceding two chapters may be said to have reached its climax about 1960. From that year, for a decade, economic growth occupied

> an exalted position in the hierarchy of goals of government policy, both in the United States and abroad, both in advanced and in less developed countries, both in centrally controlled and decentralized economies. National governments [proclaimed] target growth rates for such diverse economies as the Soviet Union, Yugoslavia, India, Sweden, France, Japan — and even for the United Kingdom and the United States, where the targets [indicated] dissatisfaction with past performance.[1]

The New Frontier

1960 was the year of the US presidential elections in which Richard Nixon defeated Nelson Rockefeller for the Republican nomination and John F. Kennedy defeated Nixon for the Presidency by 34 221 531 to 34 108 474 votes. Economic growth was a major campaign issue. The pace was set by Rockefeller who had for some years stressed its importance and now campaigned on a promise to raise American growth rates.[2] Nixon, too, favoured growth. As Eisenhower's Vice-President, he had in the previous year chaired a Cabinet Committee on Economic Growth which had placed economic growth first among the nation's economic objectives, ahead of 'maximum employment opportunities' and 'reasonable stability of the price level'. But, as a conservative Republican, he declined to join his Democratic opponents 'in playing what is rapidly becoming the most fashionable parlour game of our time — a game we might well call "growthmanship"'.[3] The Democratic platform promised a 5 per cent growth rate. When Kennedy took over the Presidency faster economic growth became a central objective, the most conspicuous signpost of the New Frontier. The first question President Kennedy put to the economist he selected as his Chairman of the Council of Economic Advisers, Walter Heller, was 'Do you think we can make good on that 5 per cent growth promise in the Democratic platform?'[4] and within a week of taking office he delivered to Congress a special message on a 'Program for Economic Recovery and Growth'.[5] The Kennedy Administration's 'commitment to growth'[6] was formally proclaimed to the world in December 1961 when it joined nineteen other member governments of the OECD in an agreement to aim at a 50 per cent growth of collective real GNP during the decade of the 1960s.[7]

Much of the impetus to economic growth in the United States continued to derive from concern for national security and from the Soviet economic challenge.[8] 'Unless we are moving here at home,' said Kennedy in one of his last election campaign speeches, 'we cannot move the cause of freedom around the world. If we lack a first rate growing economy, we cannot maintain a first rate defense'.[9] But in the last years of the 1950s, and of the Eisenhower Administration, the apparent sluggishness of the domestic economy became in the minds of many an even more urgent consideration. Successive upturns in the business cycle had become shorter, with higher unemployment percentages at successive peaks. The second half of 1960 had brought another downturn and by December the (seasonally adjusted) unemployment rate reached nearly 7 per cent.[10] Once again, as in the late 1940s, faster economic growth, all other purposes apart, came to be seen as essential to full employment. 'In the past seven years,' said Kennedy,

> our rate of growth has slowed down disturbingly... The gap between what we can produce and what we do produce has threatened to become chronic... Realistic aims for 1961 are to reverse the downward trend in our economy, to narrow the gap of unused potential, to abate the waste and misery of unemployment.[11]

'Only an economy which is realizing its potential can produce the goods and create the jobs the country needs'.[12] The UN *World Economic Survey for 1960*, with an eye very much to the situation in the United States, put the Domar–Harrod case for economic growth still more explicitly: 'What is required is not merely to maintain a high level of output but to sustain a steady rate of growth that is adequate to absorb each year's new entrants into the labour force as well as the manpower released by advancing technology and rising productivity'.[13]

While national security and full employment seemed, for the moment, the most compelling reasons for faster growth, they derived support from the many other arguments that had been developed in the preceding decade. Economic growth would 'aid in the pursuit of many other goals', including price stability and the balance of payments.[14] It was needed also to meet the manifold claims on the nation's productive capacity. As one shrewd observer put it, 'thus, anyone who favoured more foreign aid or more missiles or a quicker American appearance on the moon or urban renewal or medicare or better schools...[might] find himself urging faster economic growth upon his leaders'.[15] But he also added that these were 'only the bread-and-butter explanations of economic growth's popularity. The less tangible are conceivably the more influential explanations. One is the American tradition of expansion'. And he quoted pointedly from the Rockefeller Panel's report: 'The adventure of the American economy is a continuing reality. The dynamism that has produced the present level of well-being holds out the promise of a still more challenging future. Our nation is dedicated to economic growth'.[16]

Affirmations of this dedication came around 1960 from almost every section of organised American opinion. The Joint Economic Committee of Congress, after voluminous hearings, proclaimed a high rate of economic growth as one of the main objectives of public economic policy in its report on *Employment, Growth and Price Levels* (1960). The Chamber of Commerce of the United States published *The Promise of Economic Growth* (1960); the American Federation of Labour and Congress of Industrial Organizations, *Policies for Economic Growth* (1959); the Committee for Economic Development, *The Budget and Economic Growth* (1959); the National Planning Association, *Long-Range Projections for Economic Growth: The American Economy in 1970* (1960); and *Fortune* magazine a piece on 'How the U.S. Can Get 50 Per Cent Richer'.[17]

The only public expressions of doubt or reservation at this time came from a few social critics such as J.K. Galbraith (of whom more in chapter seven) and from conservatives fearful that too great an emphasis on growth would endanger price stability and considerably extend government control over the economy. President Eisenhower's last Economic Report (1959) outlined 'A Program for Economic Growth with Stable Prices' and the majority report of his Commission on National Goals was careful to qualify its advocacy of economic growth: 'The economy should grow at the maximum rate consistent with primary dependence upon free enterprise and the avoidance of marked inflation'.[18] Nixon, in the St Louis speech which gave birth to 'growthmanship', asserted flatly that 'there is no possibility that the Soviet economy will overtake our own any time this century', and criticised the 'growthmanship school' for arguing that 'the Government should plan and manipulate the economy to arrive at an arbitrary, fixed percentage rate of growth... They have greater faith in government action than in private enterprise as a creative force in insuring economic progress'.[19] But these conservatives were not — dared not be — against growth. 'We must never forget that growth is only one objective of national policy, though admittedly a vitally important one'.[20]

Planning for Growth

In Britain, too, the wave of enthusiasm for growth reached its crest about 1960. But in the somewhat different economic circumstances and political climate of Britain, somewhat different arguments predominated and different policy inferences were drawn.

In contrast to the American emphasis on full employment and the Soviet challenge, economic growth was here presented as the way out of the country's general economic malaise, of which creeping inflation, periodic balance of payments crises and 'stop–go' policies were seen as the most conspicuous short-run symptoms, and falling behind the countries of the European Economic Community across the Channel in productive capacity and living standards the inevitable longer-term consequence.

We noted before that, as early as 1955, some British economists were becoming impatient with a policy of periodic restraint for the sake of the balance of payments.[21]

> The boom of 1955 had been encouraged by policy; when it was reversed, policy remained restrictive for three years... After this experience, it seemed reasonable to hope that intervention on this scale could in future be avoided... Yet the expansion induced in 1958 and 1959 had to be severely checked barely fifteen months after it got under way.[22]

Objections to 'stop–go' policies now became much more wide-spread. Some economists persuaded themselves that there was no need to choose between growth and internal or external balance. On the contrary, 'in the long run, a high rate of growth *promotes* price stability'[23] and 'one of the ways of helping the expansion of exports might be to keep home demand in continuing buoyancy'.[24] Even those who were not so confident tended more and more to give growth priority over stability. 'It is dangerous for a weakly progressive economy to aim at a regime of stable prices'.[25] 'If policy is to aim at producing steady growth, it must, as it were, drive straight through fluctuations in the balance of payments'.[26]

Much of the economic part of the first debate over British entry into the European Common Market — which began in the mid-1950s with moves towards a Free Trade Area including Britain and ended with President de Gaulle's veto in January 1963 — turned on the implications for growth in the United Kingdom. The growth argument for entry was put, rather surprisingly, by Balogh in 1960: 'The real issue...is whether Britain can afford to stay out of a combination which has already proved remarkably dynamic, and which might, if we joined, inject new energy into our lethargic economy. Should we refuse, Britain risks becoming an economic backwater'.[27] Three years later he had come to fear that, if Britain entered, her economy was liable 'to be swamped rather than stimulated'[28] by the dynamism of the Common Market, and this was throughout one of the main economic arguments of the opponents, such as Kaldor, who argued that 'economic integration invariably favours the most go-ahead industrial regions... It must not be forgotten that for reasons of manpower reserve (if no other) the industries of the Six are likely to continue to grow at a faster rate than Britain'.[29] If much of the debate about entry into the EEC was 'concerned with its influence on the rate of economic growth', it was no less vigorous for the fact that this was 'a subject on which there seems to be no clear-cut empirical evidence'.[30]

Until 1961, official policy statements continued to urge the need for restraint. 'The fact that from time to time the Government are forced to restrain demand is not a contradiction of [their] general policy of encouraging economic growth'.[31] 'The growth of the economy must be interlocked with the growth of exports — otherwise the balance of payments situation is bound to frustrate growth and force a reversal of direction'.[32] In 1962 the emphasis changed. The Chancellor of the Exchequer in the Conservative government, Mr Selwyn Lloyd, responded to public demand for 'planning' which had been building up in various quarters in the preceding year or two and set up a National Economic Development Office, under a Council, promptly nicknamed 'Neddy'.

Planning, until then, had in Britain been a slogan of the socialist left, associated with extension of public ownership and direct government control over the private sector. It was now taken up by influential business voices and others who believed that 'indicative planning' of the kind practised in France since the war provided a model compatible with a mixed economy and that such planning could put an end to 'stop–go' in Britain and induce faster economic growth.[33] A conference of the Federation of British Industries held at Brighton in November 1960[34] called for a kind of indicative planning, undertaken jointly by government and industry, whose 'main aim should be economic growth'.[35] In the following months, the idea caught on. French planners were invited to London to explain to a conference organised by PEP (Political and Economic Planning) how it worked in France.[36] Economists began to argue that planning would enable the government to 'accept bigger risks with the balance of payments and the pound sterling in the short run in order to achieve a more rapid increase in Britain's productive capacity'.[37] One went so far as to insist that 'the planners must plan for a growth rate far in excess of what we have been achieving lately... The idea of overtaking the Americans in their level of productivity is by no means chimerical'.[38]

The key to 'indicative planning' was target setting, an overall GNP growth target for the economy as a whole and consistent output and investment targets for sectors and industries. The notion that such target setting would accelerate growth relied partly on a kind of 'collective auto-suggestion',[39] the idea that 'management and labour are stirred to greater efforts by being made to realise both the desirability of a high rate of growth and the possibility of achieving it',[40] and partly on belief in the efficacy of planned balanced growth, in the sense that, 'if the managers in an industry are reasonably confident that those in other industries will attempt to carry out plans consistent with their own, they may be more inclined to proceed with ambitious schemes for capital investment and innovation'.[41] The popularity which French planning enjoyed in Britain was partly based on misunderstanding. The impression that French indicative planning was essentially voluntary, dependent on persuasion and voluntary co-operation, 'planning without teeth', was largely mistaken[42] and the view that it was responsible for the relatively high rate of growth of the French economy during the 1950s at least unproven.[43] But the French model fitted the mood and therefore became influential.

The idea of a National Economic Development Council was first officially aired by Selwyn Lloyd in July 1961: 'The controversial matter of planning at once arises... I am not frightened of the word'.[44] In January 1962, having secured the agreement of the Trade Union Council to be represented, he set up the NEDC, with a National Economic Development Office secretariat. Its terms of reference were circumspectly vague: 'To study centrally the plans and prospects of our main industries, to correlate them with each other and with the public sector, and to see how in aggregate they contribute to and fit in with the prospects of the economy as a whole'.[45] At its second meeting, in May 1962, the Council instructed its secretariat to investigate the possibilities of a 4 per cent annual rate of growth over the period 1961 to 1966, half as fast again as the British growth rate during the 1950s, and to discuss its implications with a cross section of major industries.[46]

The NEDO was a semi-official body and its growth target did not obtain full official blessing until just before the 1964 elections. By contrast, the new Labour government set up a Department of Economic Affairs and instructed it to prepare a National Plan. The Plan envisaged a growth rate of GDP of 3.8 per cent per annum from 1964 to 1970.

The outcome was disappointing. The actual growth rate during 1961 to 1966 averaged 3.0 per cent and during 1964 to 1970 barely 2.5 per cent. The reasons for the failure of the NEDC and the National Plan were much discussed.

> The first mistake, which was made both by NEDO and the National Plan, was to pick a growth rate as an assumption without properly examining the means of achieving it. The Plan's choice of an overall increase in GDP of 25 per cent from 1964 to 1970 appears to have been made without any attempt to relate the growth of output to the growth of productive resources. Its underlying productivity increase of 3.4 per cent per annum was substantially in excess of the 1960–4 increase of 2.7 per cent, yet very little justification was given for it. It must be asked, however, whether enough is known about the causes of growth to establish the conditions under which an increase of this order can be expected. The answer is probably that not enough is yet known.[47]

Why Growth Rates Differ

While anxiety about lagging growth was probably greatest in the United States and United Kingdom, enthusiasm for growth was by no means confined to these two countries. And although the belief that planning would promote faster growth was widespread, it was acknowledged, at least by professional economists, that 'not enough is yet known about the causes of growth' to justify confidence in the ability of governments to accelerate growth. Out of this recognition arose a spate of studies of why growth rates differ in different countries and circumstances.

The confident mood of 1960 about economic growth as a policy objective is well illustrated by a passage in the introduction on 'Objectives and Policies for Economic Growth' to the UN *World Economic Survey for 1959:*

> The first major advance in the evolution of the economic goals of the world community was taken in relation to the achievement and maintenance of economic stability... The reinterpretation of the objective of full employment under the United Nations Charter so as to embrace the goal of economic growth marks a second fundamental change in public policy thinking. In the developed countries it [has] substituted a dynamic goal of expansion for a static goal of avoidance of depression. Increasingly it has become apparent that the realization of the goal of economic growth may render manageable the dominant economic problems, both national and international, which in a stationary economy might produce only conflict and frustration.[48]

The increasing preoccupation of European public opinion and governments with economic growth had, as a distinguished economic historian has pointed out, a transatlantic inspiration. American administrations even before 1961 did all they could to preach and promote economic growth in western Europe, partly because they saw an economically prosperous and politically united western Europe as a bulwark to communism.

> Transatlantic inspiration to European policies of growth...however, came not only from what the U.S.A. gave or preached but also from what the U.S.A. was. America's economic strength, her output and productivity, her technological achievements and ever-mounting prosperity provided Europeans with an object of emulation... Above all, American affluence and American levels of consumption — motor-cars, domestic gadgets and all — were held up as a promise of rewards to come. In short, America's very presence provided an impulse to European growth and a measure of its achievements.[49]

Not only France and Britain, Sweden and the Netherlands, but also Germany, Belgium and Switzerland which had 'remained the citadels of non-interventionist policies...took in the sixties [steps] towards a more purposeful control of economic growth'.[50] In Germany it was the slowing-down of the 'miraculous' growth of the 1950s which induced the government of Dr Erhard in 1962 to set up a Council of Economic Experts to make prognoses on medium-term trends. In Belgium, dissatisfaction with sluggish growth led in 1960 to the establishment of an office for economic programming with the role of devising policies consciously directed towards economic growth.[51] At the other end of the world, 'the National Income Doubling Plan, mapped out in 1960, proved a momentous landmark for a shift of the Japanese economy from the stage of post-war reconstruction to that of fresh development'.[52]

Strong international support for growth consciousness came from the OEEC which during the 1950s matured from its original role as an organisation for the administration of Marshall aid into an influential policy forum of the developed market economies. As early as August 1951, its secretariat had persuaded member governments to set a target for the GNP of western Europe in 1956 at a level 25 per cent higher than that of 1951.[53] The need to raise productivity, to expand production 'if Member countries are rapidly to improve their living standards in the coming years',[54] recurred as the *leitmotiv* in its reports throughout the 1950s. In 1958 the OEEC Council recommended that member countries 'should now pursue policies encouraging sustainable economic growth'.[55] In the *Eleventh Annual Economic Review* of April 1960 a new theme came to the fore: OEEC countries are now 'better placed for shouldering their responsibility for ensuring continued expansion of world trade and accelerating the development of less-advanced economies'.[56] While growth in the west would benefit the less developed countries by ensuring continued expansion of world trade, more was needed to prevent an ever widening 'gap' between rich and poor countries. In December 1960, the Organisation was renamed and reconstituted as the OECD — Organisation for Economic Co-operation *and Development*. The addition of 'Development' was primarily designed to underline the role of the Organisation, through its Development Assistance Committee, as the club of aid donor countries. But it also reflected the stress on growth as a domestic economic policy objective in the member countries. In December 1961, the ministers of member countries met for the first time.

The chief outcome of the meeting was a solemn agreement 'to set a growth target...for attainment during the decade 1960–1970 of 50 per cent in real gross national product for the twenty Member countries taken together'.[57] In 1962, the Council found that, 'while the growth target was well within the physical capabilities of Member countries, experience had already shown the need for a better and fuller use of economic resources for this purpose'.[58] Four years later the secretariat was satisfied that 'the setting of a collective target has served not only to challenge countries individually to adopt more effective policies for the promotion of economic growth. It has also facilitated the adoption of such policies by helping to create an expansive climate'.[59]

Among the means of achieving a better use of economic resources for growth was widely, though by no means unanimously, believed to be some kind of long-term planning. By 1960, France, Norway, the Netherlands and Sweden had completed three four-year plans. In the following years, Belgium and the United Kingdom, Ireland and Iceland, as well as all the less developed countries of southern Europe, established some kind of long-term planning or at least machinery for producing such a plan.[60] The trend towards long-term planning was seen as reflecting 'the quest for rationality and continuity in economic policy-making' and, more specifically, 'gradual recognition of the need for a more active role of the government' and 'growing preoccupation with long-term objectives', not least 'concern for rapid growth'.[61] When the United Nations General Assembly in December 1961 requested the Secretary-General 'to provide studies of planning techniques under various economic and social systems', it was hoping mainly for guidance to the UN regional institutes for economic development and planning that were being set up in the less developed regions,[62] but its resolution also signalled the vogue of planning which was a feature of the high tide of growth consciousness in the developed countries.

Even supporters of planning, or at least the more sophisticated among them, realised that 'rationality and continuity in policy-making' alone would not guarantee more rapid economic growth. What policies were most likely to accelerate growth? What factors promote, what factors impede growth? Why had some countries, most conspicuously Japan and Germany, but also France and Italy, been growing so much faster than Britain, the USA, Belgium and Ireland?

The study of these questions became in the early 1960s a major research interest of international agencies, research institutes and individual scholars in western countries. The ultimate purpose of all these studies was, in the blunt words of the first of them to appear, Angus Maddison's *Economic Growth in the West,* to throw light on 'the problem of how the rich countries can get richer'.[63] But in the process, much effort and ingenuity was devoted to scholarly comparison and analysis of the growing volume of data that was becoming available on the growth performance of different countries. The UN *World Economic Survey for 1959* contained a preliminary study on these lines and Part 2 of the *Economic Survey of Europe in 1961* (publication of which was delayed until 1964), a more extensive one.[64] In 1967, the Brookings Institution published E.F. Denison's sophisticated analysis of *Why Growth Rates Differ.*[65]

The most important single conclusion which emerged from all these studies was a negative one. Only a small part of differences among countries in growth performance could be accounted for by differences in rates of factor input, capital formation and growth in the labour force.[66] The conclusion led to a search for better understanding of the 'residual factor'.[67] One result was a downgrading of the importance for growth attributed for so long to fixed capital formation and greater emphasis on investment in 'human capital' through education, and on other still less tangible factors. For those who had hoped for results from these studies which could be readily applied in policies for faster growth the outcome was chastening. By the end of the 1960s it still seemed that 'not enough is yet known about the causes of growth' to put governments and their planners on the right track.

References

1 James Tobin, 'Economic Growth as an Objective of Government Policy', *American Economic Review*, May 1964 (AEA Proceedings), p. 1.

2 R. Lekachman, *The Age of Keynes* (Allen Lane, London, 1966), p. 178.

3 R.M. Nixon, speech at St Louis, *New York Times*, 22 June 1960, p. 28. Robert Solow has suggested that the clever adaptation of Stephen Potter may have been due to President Eisenhower's special assistant, Allen Wallis ('Economic Growth', in P.M. Gutmann [ed.], *Economic Growth: An American Problem* [Prentice-Hall, Englewood Cliffs, N.J., 1964], p. 101).

4 W.W. Heller, *Perspectives on Economic Growth* (Random House, New York, 1968), p. ix.

5 E.S. Flash, *Economic Advice and Presidential Leadership* (Columbia University Press, New York, 1965), p. 180.

6 Heller, *op. cit.*, p. xii.

7 *Ibid.*, p. 3.

8 Cf., e.g., K. Knorr and W.J. Baumol (eds), *What Price Economic Growth?* (Prentice-Hall, Englewood Cliffs, N.J., 1961); but also A.H. Hansen, *Economic Issues of the 1960s* (McGraw Hill, New York, 1960).

9 Knorr and Baumol, *op. cit.*, p. 2.

10 Flash, *op. cit.*, p. 181.

11 Lekachman, *op. cit.*, p. 178.

12 W.W. Heller, quoted in Flash, *op. cit.*, p. 190.

13 United Nations, *World Economic Survey for 1960* (New York, 1961), p. 5.

14 Heller, *op. cit.*, p. ix.

15 Lekachman, *op. cit.*, p. 179.

16 *Ibid.*

17 The list of references is taken from Knorr and Baumol, *op. cit.*, p. 2.

18 The American Assembly, *Goals for Americans* (Prentice-Hall, Englewood Cliffs, N.J., 1960), p. 10. Clark Kerr and George Meany dissented from this recommendation; the latter claiming that 'the nation clearly can, should and must grow at an annual rate of 4.5–5 per cent' (*ibid.*, p. 29).

19 R.M. Nixon, *loc. cit.* American Liberals agreed; cf. Alvin Hansen: 'Basically the matter simmers down to this: under currently dominant political tenets, the Federal government is not permitted to play the role which is requisite for adequate growth' (Hansen, *op. cit.*, p. 44).

20 R.M. Nixon, *loc. cit.*

21 See ch. 4, p. 44.

22 J.C.R. Dow, *The Management of the British Economy 1945–60* (Cambridge University Press, Cambridge, 1964), p. 111.

23 P. Streeten and T. Balogh, 'A Reconsideration of Monetary Policy', *Bulletin*, Oxford Institute of Statistics, November 1957, quoted in T.W. Hutchison, *Economics and Economic Policy in Britain 1946–66* (Allen & Unwin, London, 1968), p. 151.

24 R.F. Harrod, in *The Director*, August 1961, quoted in Hutchison, *op. cit.*, p. 218.

25 N. Kaldor, in *The Times*, 19 October 1962, quoted in Hutchison, *op. cit.*, p. 204.

26 Dow, *op. cit.*, p. 399.

27 T. Balogh, in *New Statesman and Nation*, 21 May 1960, quoted in Hutchison, *op. cit.*, pp. 193–4.

28 T. Balogh, *Unequal Partners* (Blackwell, Oxford, 1963), vol. 2, p. 270.

29 N. Kaldor, *loc. cit.*

30 H.G. Johnson, 'The Criteria of Economic Advantage', in G.D.N. Worswick (ed.), *The Free Trade Proposals* (Blackwell, Oxford, 1960), quoted in Hutchison, *op. cit.*, p. 195.

31 *Economic Survey for 1961*, Cmd 1334, HMSO, London, 1961, pp. 9–10.

32 *Ibid.*

33 On the planning experiments in Britain in the 1960s, see T. Wilson, *Planning and Growth* (Macmillan, London, 1965), ch. 1; Hutchison, *op. cit.*, pp. 183–90; E.E. Hagen and S.F.T. White, *Great Britain: Quiet Revolution in Planning* (Syracuse University Press, Syracuse, N.Y., 1966).

34 Hutchison, *op. cit.*, p. 185; Colin Clark, *Growthmanship* (Hobart Papers No. 10, 2nd edn, Institute of Economic Affairs, London, 1962), p. 10.

35 Hutchison, *op. cit.*, p. 185.

36 *Economic Planning in France* (PEP, August 1961): this report was edited by J.C.R. Dow (see Dow, *op. cit.*, p. 399); J. and A.M. Hackett, *Economic Planning in France* (Allen & Unwin, London, 1963).

37 A. Shonfield, in *The Observer*, 15 January 1961, quoted in Clark, *op. cit.*, p. 10.

38 R.F. Harrod, 'The Significance of Planning', *District Bank Review*, December 1961, p. 21.

39 Hutchison, *op. cit.*, p. 208.

40 Wilson, *op. cit.*, pp. 37–8.

41 *Ibid.*, p. 38.

42 *Ibid.*, p. 40.

43 United Nations Economic Commission for Europe, *Some Factors in Economic Growth in Europe during the 1950s* (Geneva, 1964), ch. 6, p. 15.

44 Quoted in Dow, *op. cit.*, p. 398.

45 *Ibid.*, p. 399.

46 *Ibid.*

47 M.C. Kennedy, 'The Economy as a Whole', in A.R. Prest (ed.), *The UK Economy: A Manual of Applied Economics* (3rd edn, Weidenfeld & Nicolson, London, 1970), p. 45.

48 United Nations, *World Economic Survey for 1959* (New York, 1960), p. 5.

49 M.M. Postan, *An Economic History of Western Europe 1945–1964* (Methuen, London, 1967), p. 49.

50 *Ibid.*, p. 42.

51 *Ibid.*, pp. 42 ff.

52 Saburo Okita, *Japan in the World Economy* (The Japan Foundation, Tokyo, June 1975), pp. 6–7.

53 *Sixth Report of the OEEC* (OEEC, Paris, March 1955), vol. 1, p. 16.

54 *Ibid.*, p. 175.

55 *Tenth Annual Economic Review* (OEEC, Paris, March 1959), p. 51.

56 *Eleventh Annual Economic Review* (OEEC, Paris, April 1960), p. 7.

57 *OECD* (OECD, Paris, 1963), p. 16.

58 *Ibid.*

59 *Economic Growth 1960–1970* (OECD, Paris, 1966), p. 7.

60 United Nations Economic Commission for Europe, *Economic Planning in Europe* (Geneva, 1965), ch. 1, p. 1.

61 *Ibid.*, p. 2.

62 *Ibid.*, p. iii.

63 A. Maddison, *Economic Growth in the West* (Allen & Unwin, London, 1964), p. 16.

64 *Some Factors in Economic Growth in Europe during the 1950s*, ch. 6, p. 15.

65 (Washington, 1967); cf. also E.F. Denison, *The Sources of Economic Growth in the United States* (Committee for Economic Development, New York, 1962).

66 One of the first to put this view was Colin Clark (*Growthmanship*, pp. 25 ff.); cf. also O. Aukrust, 'Investment and Economic Growth', *Productivity Measurement Review*, February 1959.

67 Cf. *The Residual Factor in Economic Growth* (OECD, Paris, 1964).

6 The Full Case for Economic Growth

The preceding chapters have tried to trace the rise of economic growth to pre-eminence among policy objectives. This historical approach has probably failed to do justice to the case for economic growth. It has unavoidably emphasised the pressures and rationalisations dictated at various times by the most urgent problems of the day. What has emerged must seem to advocates of economic growth a statement of their view thin at best and bordering on caricature at worst. It may therefore be desirable to pause at this point of the historical narrative to restate the full case for economic growth as it was presented by its more thoughtful proponents in its heyday.

Material Progress

Behind all the special pleadings for economic growth there lay an assumption so much taken for granted that it was not always made explicit — a largely 'inarticulate major premise', as Professor Laski would have called it — modern western man's belief in the desirability of material progress. Not everyone, but the great majority, favoured a high rate of economic growth basically because they regarded 'a sustained rise in material standards as wholly desirable'.[1]

'For the vast majority of mankind — who live in the underdeveloped areas of Asia, Africa and Latin America — the question why economic growth is desirable' seemed 'almost frivolous. For them, the most rapid possible rise in per capita income means, immediately, no more than emancipation from abject poverty, squalor, drudgery and disease'. 'In the relatively much richer industrial countries of Europe and North America, the case for putting rapid growth high among the objectives of economic policy' was conceded to be less obvious... The fastest growing economies of Europe — such as the Soviet Union — would, if they maintained their present rates of growth, double their levels of per capita income every nine years, which would mean a 2,000-fold increase over a hundred years. It may well be asked why continuing rapid growth should be regarded as an important objective in these countries. Looking a hundred years ahead, the question does not perhaps admit of a ready answer. But if the question relates only to the next decade or generation, there are a number of answers.[2]

One was the answer given, in hyperbole, by Samuelson in 1948 and already quoted: 'Even the richest of such nations, the United States, would have to be hundreds of times more productive than it is now to give everybody as comfortable a standard of living as is now enjoyed by our most fortunate few'.[3] The UN Report put the same point more moderately:

Even in the relatively well-to-do countries, standards of living are far from ideal... There are few, even among the upper income groups, in these countries who would not be conscious of some benefit from further increase in their real personal incomes; and it will require large increases in national productive capacities to raise the lower income groups in the same countries to the standards of material comfort now enjoyed by the fortunate minority.[4]

Disdain for material progress was easy for the well-to-do. 'Those enjoying an above-average standard of living should be rather chary of admonishing those less fortunate on the perils of material riches'.[5]

Even had it been granted that there was little to be said for efforts to raise average real *personal* consumption in the rich countries much further, there remained a case for rapid growth of productive capacity in these countries to raise their own standards of social and other public expenditure and their capacity to help promote higher living standards in poorer countries.

In many [well-to-do] countries, those elements in consumers' welfare provided through public expenditures have become increasingly inadequate... There are vast needs for housing, city planning, medical services, education and cultural facilities which could absorb, for the next ten to twenty years, a large part of the increment of per capita production yielded by economic growth at present rates.

At the same time, 'the volume of aid to the developing countries which the already well-to-do countries will be able to supply will depend in no small measure on the rate of domestic economic growth the latter can achieve'.[6]

The more sophisticated advocates of economic growth for higher living standards did not argue their case on crudely hedonistic grounds. As Arthur Lewis said, in one of the first, and still one of the best, statements of the case,

> the advantage of economic growth is not that wealth increases happiness, but that it increases the range of human choice... We certainly cannot say that an increase in wealth makes people happier. We cannot say, either, that an increase in wealth makes people less happy, and even if we could say this, it would not be a decisive argument against economic growth, since happiness is not the only good thing in life. We do not know what the purpose of life is, but if it were happiness, then evolution might just as well have stopped a long time ago, since there is no reason to believe that men are happier than pigs or than fishes. What distinguishes men from pigs is that men have greater control over their environment; not that they are more happy. And on this test, economic growth is greatly to be desired. The case for economic growth is that it gives man greater control over his environment, and thereby increases his freedom.[7]

Lewis was thinking of the very poor in less developed countries, those 'regularly visited by famine, plague or pestilence'.[8] But much the same case was made also for economic growth in post-war England: 'One cannot state dogmatically that rising material standards...will make people "happier". I personally think that they probably will... Whatever the effects of rising standards on happiness, they clearly increase the individual's range of choice and area of cultural possibilities'.[9]

In any case, whether or not economic growth makes people happy, and however much we may 'deplore the fact (if it is a fact) that this virtue [of economy] is found only in association with the vice (if it is a vice) of materialism', the fact is that 'man likes to have more wealth, likes to economize, and likes to be idle'.[10] At the most pragmatic level, whatever may be thought 'by writers and intellectuals, the people themselves are quite determined on a rapid improvement in their living standards; and governments will have to attend to their wishes'.[11] 'British society, for the present at least, does attach considerable importance to "the material results of growth"'.[12] 'Moreover, many would probably prefer continually rising consumption to stability even at a tolerable level of affluence'.[13]

Competing Claims

Far from feeling concern about the satiability of wants and the futility of affluence, people and governments in western countries felt oppressed by a burden of competing claims on limited resources from which more rapid economic growth of productive capacity seemed the only escape. In the fully employed post-war economy there were 'no easy reserves waiting to be tapped... Improved living standards, or any other economic claims, can now be met only by higher production per head'.[14] And of other claims there seemed no end.

We noted before the Douglas Committee's *cri de coeur*: 'The critical need for economic growth is found in the tasks placed upon the nation, both foreign and domestic. At no time has any free nation been faced with a greater call upon its resources than the United States today'.[15] There is the task of defence. 'The United States must bear the major responsibility for protecting the free world from the threat of Communist aggression.' There is aid. 'The United States will have to continue to assume considerable responsibility for providing economic aid to speed up the economic development of the underdeveloped countries.' At home, there are the requirements of a rapidly growing population for services which can only be, or are most effectively, provided by government. 'We must devote both a larger amount and a larger share of our resources to educate the growing population of young people.' Even in the rich United States there are pockets of severe poverty. 'While economic growth does reduce some poverty as incomes rise, certain groups, including those out of the labour force for reasons of age or disability, minorities who suffer from discrimination in their access to jobs, migrant farm workers, and American Indians are bypassed by economic progress.' Then there are the problems of urban growth, the need for 'such programs as slum clearance and the improvement and expansion of public utilities'. Clearly, 'a high rate of economic growth is essential if these public responsibilities are to be discharged without limiting the advance in living standards effected through individual efforts'.[16]

The simple arithmetic that a high rate of growth in gross national product makes it possible to enlarge both private income per head and public outlays — 'the higher the growth rate, the less the potential clash between the claims of the two sectors'[17] — had a wider application to the problem of competing income claims between labour and capital and other social groups. The struggle over shares among all sections of western communities came increasingly, during the 1950s and 1960s, to be recognised as a major source of chronic and accelerating inflation.

Perhaps no other argument appealed more to thoughtful people, on the left as on the right, than that economic growth may, in Galbraith's paraphrase, prove to be 'the great solvent of the tensions associated with inequality'.[18] Galbraith himself, writing in 1957, thought the facts inescapable: 'It is the increase in output in recent decades, not the redistribution of income, which has brought the great material increase, the well-being of the average man'.[19] Many would have been prepared to echo A.G.B. Fisher's sentiments quoted in an earlier chapter: 'The gross inequalities of capitalist society, if they are to be justified at all, can find justification' only in the promise of rising average living standards and vertical mobility —

> in the belief that sufficient plasticity and flexibility are maintained to make possible a steady if irregular improvement in the standard of living, while at the same time opportunities are offered from time to time to individuals to transfer to departments of work where the level of remuneration is higher.[20]

The belief that steadily, rapidly and (at least for the foreseeable future) indefinitely increasing productive capacity is an important policy objective even in the rich countries because higher living standards in the widest sense are desirable and demanded, undoubtedly constituted the core of the case for economic growth. But this central proposition was reinforced by a variety of other considerations which, while not on their own enough to sustain a high priority for economic growth, were more than mere rationalisations or debating points of growthmanship.

Making Other Problems More Manageable

'Economic growth may render manageable the dominant economic problems, both national and international, which in a stationary economy might produce only conflict and frustration'.[21]

The argument that a growing economy afforded more scope than a stationary one for softening and deflecting the struggle over competing income claims among social groups and that rapid economic growth should therefore help keep the problem of inflation within bounds was one example. As regards problems of external balance, it was generally recognised that rapid economic growth was liable to aggravate rather that alleviate one's own country's balance of payments deficit, but it was argued, plausibly, that balance of payments adjustment would be easier all round, and competition for export markets less acrimonious, in an expanding world economy.[22] By far the most important and influential illustration of the general proposition, however, was the importance attributed to growth as a necessary means to full employment.

Since there were so many other good reasons for favouring economic growth, no one was particularly concerned to examine whether there was any escape from the logic of the Harrod–Domar theorem that 'the preservation of full employment in a capitalist economy requires a growing income',[23] to enquire, for example, whether any modern industrial society, capitalist or socialist, could operate in stationary conditions, with zero net saving. At the level of practical policy, there was no gainsaying the fact that, most conspicuously in the United States but potentially in all the mixed economies, sluggish growth was contributing to unemployment and excess capacity and that, if for no other reason, an adequate rate of economic growth was desirable 'to absorb each year's new entrants into the labour force as well as the manpower released by advancing technology and rising productivity'.[24] Certainly, it was not unreasonable to attach weight in the mix of policy objectives to 'the assurance provided by growth against the danger of Keynesian stagnation and unemployment'.[25]

Yet another way in which economic growth, it was claimed, would help render other problems more manageable was the greater ease of adjustment to structural change in a growing economy. Changes in demand and technology are more easily accommodated if no sectors or industries face absolute decline but at worst slower expansion than others. More generally, 'the greater flexibility of an expanding economy...means more freedom of manoeuvre for individuals and groups and less risk of the social hardships incidental to change'.[26]

The Cheerful State

One cannot re-read the growth literature of the 1950s and 1960s without being struck by the number of writers who, unabashedly or shamefacedly, confessed to sharing Adam Smith's view of the progressive state as 'the cheerful and hearty state to all the different orders of the society'.[27] Those who remembered the 'economic lethargy of the 1950s'[28] preferred to put up with 'the problems and difficulties of growth, instead of the incomparably more morbid symptoms of stagnation and decay'.[29] A not insignificant element in the advocacy of growth, as Samuelson has pointed out, was 'the belief that, even if more material goods are not themselves most important, nevertheless, a society is happier when it is moving forward and is unhappy when it is stagnating and beset by protectionist and other movements that thrive in such an environment'.[30]

In the United States, as we noted before, belief in economic growth had something of the status of a national faith, proclaimed the more ardently when it seemed in danger of being lost. 'The adventure of the American economy is a continuing reality'.[31] Hardly less committedly, Domar, having observed that 'as a goal of economic policy, growth has absorbed some of the public attention previously enjoyed by full employment', declared growth to be 'the healthier objective not only because it implies a rising standard of living, which is obvious, but also because it thrives on saving, ingenuity, efficiency, good management, hard work, and other good and puritanical virtues'.[32]

In the older countries of Europe, economic dynamism for its own sake evoked less exuberance. But here, too, there were some who were prepared to argue for economic growth on quite non-material grounds.

> Finally, growth of productive capacity — even if not of actual output of goods and services — is a precondition of rising living standards in the form of increases in leisure with no sacrifice of actual material comfort; and it may also be inferred from history that growth, in at least this sense, is bound up with many of the values of civilized life — opportunities for initiative and achievement, intellectual ferment and the advancement of knowledge.[33]

Keeping Up

Any summary of the case for economic growth, as it developed in the post-war years, would be incomplete without some reference to the role played by international rivalry.

A less laudable consideration contributing to the current emphasis on rapid economic growth even in developed countries is, of course, international and ideological rivalry. Performance in economic growth has become a matter of prestige, both for individual nations and for rival economic systems. Inter-acting with real or presumed defence and power implications of economic growth, such motives have given rapid growth a status among the objectives of economic policy of the major (and even many minor) powers almost independent of rational assessment of benefits in terms of standards of living.[34]

Fear of falling behind was, in a world of nation states, not perhaps a laudable but certainly not an entirely irrational motive for favouring economic growth, and in some circumstances more rapid economic growth. It is easy, after a generation of successful nuclear deterrence and more than a decade of Sino–Soviet hostility, to smile indulgently or scoff contemptuously at the excesses of cold war fears in western countries during the 1950s. There were also perhaps grounds for scepticism about the Soviet challenge as justifying or demanding extreme exertions for faster economic growth: 'Even if one really believes that the West will eventually be outstripped in total industrial output (which I do not), would this in fact revolutionise the balance of military power?'[35] 'On the score of national strength, there is a case for growth. But it is more subtle than the facile association of military power with generalized civilian economic capacity'.[36] But except for those optimistic enough to assume that the world had outgrown international and ideological rivalry, there was more than a grain of truth in the Wiles logic that 'in the end the country that grows most becomes biggest, and every economic advantage belongs to it, be it military power, dominance in world markets, or even a high standard of living'.[37] Obsession with international growth league tables may have reached absurd lengths in the 1960s, but it was not entirely silly for people to feel that there was something wrong, and to find it wounding to their collective self-esteem, if their own country was performing conspicuously less well than others in an area of endeavour which all regarded as important and worthwhile.

The Optimum Rate of Growth

To say that economic growth was desirable was asking merely for a rate of economic growth above zero. Most advocates of growth wanted more, but few were very specific: 'Faster' growth,[38] 'a high rate',[39] 'rapid growth',[40] 'a higher rate'.[41] Some, in moments of enthusiasm, demanded 'as much growth as possible',[42] 'growth in accordance with the maximum potential',[43] a rate 'far in excess of what we have achieved lately',[44] or whatever rate will realise the nation's 'full potentialities for growth'.[45] Some of those fearful of the Soviet challenge demanded, explicitly or implicitly, a rate of growth which would 'keep the gap between us and them as great as it is now',[46] leaving it to their leaders to guess whether the gap was to be interpreted absolutely or proportionately.

More realistic advice to governments was to try to raise the rate somewhat, and this is what governments sought to do when they set themselves growth targets. President Kennedy was advised that a rate of 4 to 5 per cent should be possible 'rather than the rate of little more than 2 per cent of recent years' and that 3.5 per cent was necessary to prevent unemployment from increasing.[47] His party platform, as we saw, promised 5 per cent.[48] The British National Plan aimed to raise the annual growth rate of GNP from 3 to about 4 per cent. The OECD's collective targets were designed, as we have seen, to be 'within the physical capabilities of Member countries' but 'challenging'.[49]

Economists discussed the 'optimum' rate of economic growth, but in terms remote from the real world. In line with prevailing doctrine which treated the rate of growth as a function of the rate of capital formation, they tended to start from the proposition that 'the question of growth is nothing new, but a new disguise for an age-old issue...the present versus the future'.[50] The argument initially revolved around the 'voluntary saving rate' as the benchmark. Those favouring a higher rate of growth would argue for 'raising the saving rate above that of voluntary saving'.[51] Others would insist that 'the "right" or optimum rate of growth is that rate which conforms to the voluntary choices of the people, rather than a rate obtained by coercion, compulsion or excessive social costs'.[52] It was then pointed out that 'we cannot escape considering growth, or more precisely, intertemporal choice as an issue of public economic policy...[since] we cannot assume either that the market settles the issue optimally or that government can be guided by some simple rules of neutrality',[53] and that the proper procedure is to ascertain by econometric analysis whether 'the returns to a higher saving and investment ratio would be positive, if evaluated by a reasonable set of social time preference interest rates'.[54] An initial attempt yielded 'evidence that policy to accelerate growth, to move the economy to a higher path, would pay.'[55] It is hardly surprising that so abstract an approach did not, even remotely, influence policy thinking.

Discussion at a more practical level centred, sensibly and inevitably, on 'the maximum rate of economic growth consistent with'[56] due regard for all other economic and non-economic ends considered important — whether it was 'primary dependence upon private enterprise and the avoidance of marked inflation'[57] or balance of payments equilibrium, defence, social justice, the rights of individuals or of trade unions or whatever. Such an approach implied recognition of the fact that the 'optimum' rate of growth depends on value judgments about the preferred mix or trade-off among conflicting objectives, in other words about the costs of growth.

The Costs of Growth

The very first considered post-war statement of the case for economic growth began with the words: 'Like everything else, economic growth has its costs. If economic growth could be achieved without any disadvantages, everybody would be wholly in its favour'.[58] And it concluded: 'The rate of economic growth can be too high for the health of society. Economic growth is only one good thing among many, and we can take it to excess'.[59] Some subsequent statements, even by professional economists, were certainly less judicious, and there is no question that growthmanship in the public and political arena for a time attached a weight to the rate of growth of GNP relative to all other policy objectives which, to most thoughtful people, would seem unreasonable. But it would be unhistorical and unfair to the advocates of economic growth of the 1950s and 1960s to end this summary of their case without a reminder about the qualifications which most of them attached to it.

Vice-President Nixon in 1960 was admittedly a somewhat lukewarm protagonist for economic growth, but when he warned that 'we must never forget that growth is only one objective of national policy'[60] he was making a point which is echoed in every significant exposition of the case for economic growth. The key issue, said one, is to decide 'how much should be sacrificed in other directions for the sake of how much more growth'.[61] 'There is,' said another, 'no call to become obsessed by it, or to strain every nerve to get the maximum rate of growth at almost any cost'.[62] 'In rich industrial countries,' said a third, 'it may not be irrational to forgo, as a matter of considered choice, some of the extra rate of growth that might be achieved by partial sacrifice of other objectives and values — security, leisure, social justice, economic equality, freedom, or a traditional way of life'.[63]

In current policy discussions, as we saw in earlier chapters, policy objectives which were most obviously seen as liable to conflict with faster economic growth were internal and external balance. Even if it was conceded that 'in the long run a high rate of growth *promotes* price stability',[64] it was evident that running an already booming economy 'at a greater pressure of demand would not in fact increase sustainable growth',[65] but would almost certainly cause or accelerate inflation. And there could be legitimate doubts about the wisdom and practicality of going for growth by 'driving straight through fluctuations in the balance of payments'.[66] In more considered statements of the case for economic growth, non-economic considerations were given more attention.

How far should western countries be prepared to go in adapting their economic and political systems to meet the Soviet challenge? Nixon committed himself to the proposition that 'what best promotes freedom best promotes growth'.[67] Others were not so sanguine:

It might be that if we closed the (presumed) gap between British and Soviet rates of growth, we should increase the degree of satisfaction of material wants. But we might do so only at the cost of very unpleasant repercussions elsewhere. It might require, for example, a great increase in inequality in order to strengthen incentives: or direction of labour, and the withdrawal of the right to strike: or a heavy sacrifice of leisure, or culture, or simply peace of mind. All this is particularly relevant since an authoritarian regime starts off with obvious advantages from the point of view of growth. It has neither free Trade Unions to contest its wage and price policy, nor free electorates to impede its fiscal policy. But this is not a sufficient argument for abandoning democracy in favour of dictatorship: on the contrary, most people would consider it an overwhelming argument against giving growth an overriding priority on grounds of economic welfare.[68]

Is 'more inequality a price that should be paid for faster growth'? In Britain, 'growth might be stimulated by reducing the taxes that penalise marginal effort and saving... Such a change would undoubtedly be opposed in Britain if it were feared that equality was being sacrificed even marginally'.[69] When the Rockefeller Panel proclaimed flatly that 'economic growth is meaningless if its benefits are not generally shared,'[70] it could be interpreted as favouring some sacrifice of growth for the sake of equality or a determined effort to combine stimulus to overall economic growth with measures to promote an equitable distribution of the benefits of growth. Unfortunately, the benefits and the costs of economic growth do not accrue necessarily — indeed accrue rarely — to the same people. 'The rate of growth will not be increased by wishing. Steps will have to be taken to increase it. By and large these steps will involve some cost to someone... Whether the benefits are worth the costs can be answered only by those affected or' — whether those affected agree or not — 'by those making the decisions'.[71]

Although economists raised and discussed the question, 'Growth in What?', it is fair criticism that, in their concern for a high rate of growth of GNP, they did not, generally, give sufficient emphasis to questions about the desirable composition of GNP. The same can be said about the hidden costs, the external diseconomies, of economic growth. They were not neglected. Arthur Lewis in 1954 discussed the argument that 'any expectation that all the nations of the world can raise their standards of living continuously must be illusory, since the effect would be only to exhaust rapidly the world's accumulated stocks of minerals and fuel'.[72] He pointed out that this argument rests upon two uncertain assumptions, first that human ingenuity must in due course fail to find new substitutes for what is used up, and second that future generations have an equal claim to the world's resources. 'Why should we stay poor so that the life of the human race may in some centuries to come be extended for a further century or so?'[73] Similarly, the Rockefeller Panel in 1958 stressed that 'any serious effort to project our growth potential for the future must take account of our supply of natural resources'.[74] But such references are rare before 1965.

Enough has been said, however, to show that economists were well enough aware of the fact that economic growth has its costs, that the only question worth asking is whether faster growth 'is sufficiently desirable to justify any particular step that might be taken to achieve it'.[75] No economist was foolish enough to think of economic growth as an 'end in itself' (though one of them used the phrase once in contrast with treating growth merely as a means to full employment).[76] 'A high rate of economic growth is...an essentially subordinate aim of policy, which should be pursued not for its own sake, but as a means to certain ends'.[77]

What many of them did think was that 'in the West, although growth has its price, that price may not be so terribly high after all'.[78]

References

1 C.A.R. Crosland, *The Future of Socialism* (Jonathan Cape, London, 1956), p. 292.

2 United Nations Economic Commission for Europe, *Some Factors in Economic Growth in Europe during the 1950s* (Geneva, 1964), ch. 1, p. 2 (hereafter cited as *Some Factors*).

3 P. Samuelson, *Economics* (1st edn, McGraw Hill, New York, 1948), p. 16.

4 *Some Factors*, p. 2.

5 Crosland, *op. cit.*, p. 292.

6 *Some Factors*, pp. 2–3.

7 W.A. Lewis, *The Theory of Economic Growth* (Allen & Unwin, London, 1955), Appendix: 'Is Economic Growth Desirable?', pp. 420–1.

8 *Ibid.*

9 Crosland, *op. cit.*, p. 290.

10 Lewis, *op. cit.*, p. 425.

11 Crosland, *op. cit.*, p. 378.

12 P.D. Henderson, 'Growth and the Balance of Payments: Some Comments', *Bulletin*, Oxford Institute of Statistics, February 1955, p. 77.

13 T. Wilson, *Planning and Growth* (Macmillan, London, 1965), p. 70.

14 Crosland, *op. cit.*, p. 376.

15 Joint Economic Committee on Employment, Growth and Price Levels (Douglas Committee), *Report* (US Congress, Washington, 1960), p. 11.

16 *Ibid.*

17 W.W. Rostow, 'America's Answer to the Soviet Challenge', in M.C. Grossman et al. (eds.), *Readings in Current Economics* (rev. edn, Irwin, Homewood, Ill., 1961), p. 458.

18 J.K. Galbraith, *The Affluent Society* (Penguin, London, 1962), pp. 86–7.

19 *Ibid.*

20 A.G.B. Fisher, *The Clash between Progress and Security* (Macmillan, London, 1935), p. 4.

21 United Nations, *World Economic Survey for 1959* (New York, 1960), p. 5.

22 Cf. United Nations Economic Commission for Europe, *Economic Survey of Europe in 1949* (Geneva, 1950), p. iii.

23 E.D. Domar, *Essays in the Theory of Economic Growth* (Oxford University Press, New York, 1957), p. 71.

24 United Nations, *World Economic Survey for 1960* (New York, 1961), p. 5.

25 *Some Factors*, p. 3.

26 *Ibid.*

27 Adam Smith, *The Wealth of Nations* (ed. E. Cannan, University Paperbacks, London, 1961), vol.1, p. 91.

28 United Nations, *World Economic Survey for 1955* (New York, 1956), p. 17.

29 John Strachey, *Labour's Task* (Fabian Tract No. 290, London, October 1951), p. 8.

30 P. Samuelson, *Economics* (6th edn, McGraw Hill, New York, 1964), p. 778.

31 *Prospect for America* (Rockefeller Panel Reports, Doubleday, New York, 1961), p. 261.

32 Domar, *op. cit.*, p. 14.

33 *Some Factors*, p. 3.

34 *Ibid.*

35 Crosland, *op. cit.*, p. 383.

36 James Tobin, 'Economic Growth as an Objective of Government Policy', in W.W. Heller, *Perspectives on Economic Growth* (Random House, New York, 1968), p. 94.

37 P.D. Wiles, 'The Soviet Economy Outpaces the West', *Foreign Affairs*, July 1953, p. 566.

38 E.g., K. Knorr and W.J. Baumol (eds), *What Price Economic Growth?* (Prentice-Hall, Englewood Cliffs, N.J., 1961), p. 1.

39 E.g., Henderson, *op. cit.*, p. 75.

40 E.g., Crosland, *op. cit.*, p. 375.

41 E.g., Rostow, *op. cit.*, p. 458.

42 R.F. Harrod, quoted in T.W. Hutchison, *Economics and Economic Policy and Britain 1946–1966* (Allen & Unwin, London, 1968), p. 185.

43 R.F. Harrod, *ibid*, p. 208.

44 R.F. Harrod, *ibid.*

45 *The Economic Implications of Full Employment*, Cmd 9725, HMSO, London, March 1956, p. 10.

46 Wiles, *op. cit.*, p. 580.

47 S.E. Harris, *The Economics of the Political Parties* (Macmillan, New York, 1962), p. 221.

48 Heller, *op. cit.*, p. ix.

49 *OECD* (OECD, Paris, 1963), p. 16, and *Economic Growth 1960–1970* (OECD, Paris, 1966), p. 7.

50 Tobin, *op. cit.*, pp. 87–8.

51 W.J. Fellner, 'Rapid Growth as an Objective of Economic Policy', *AEA Proceedings*, 1960, p. 99.

52 W.A. Wallis, 'United States Growth: What, Why, How', in E.S. Phelps, *The Goal of Economic Growth* (rev. edn, Norton, New York, 1969), p. 69.

53 Tobin, *op. cit.*, p. 105.

54 *Ibid.*, p. 110.

55 *Ibid.*

56 The American Assembly, *Goals for Americans* (Prentice-Hall, Englewood Cliffs, N.J., 1960), p. 10.

57 *Ibid.*

58 Lewis, *op. cit.*, p. 420.

59 *Ibid.*, p. 429.

60 R.M. Nixon, speech at St Louis, *New York Times*, 22 June 1960.

61 Wilson, *op. cit.*, p. 70.

62 Crosland, *op. cit.*, p. 380.

63 *Some Factors*, p. 3.

64 T. Balogh and P.P. Streeten, quoted in T.W. Hutchison, *Economics and Economic Policy in Britain 1946–66* (Allen & Unwin, London, 1968), p. 264.

65 *Economic Survey for 1961*, Cmd 1334, HMSO, London, 1961, p. 9.

66 J.C.R. Dow, *The Management of the British Economy 1945–60* (Cambridge University Press, Cambridge, 1964), p. 399.

67 R.M. Nixon, *op. cit.*

68 Crosland, *op. cit.*, p. 382.

69 Wilson, *op. cit.*, p. 72.

70 *Prospect for America, op. cit.*, p. 254.

71 H. Stein and E.F. Denison, 'Economic Growth as a National Goal', in Phelps, *op. cit.*, p. 49.

72 Lewis, *op. cit.*, p. 424.

73 *Ibid.*

74 *Prospect for America, op. cit.*, p. 286.

75 Stein and Denison, *op. cit.*, p. 49.

76 Domar, *op. cit.*, p. 5.

77 Henderson, *op. cit.*, p. 78.

78 Wilson, *op. cit.*, p. 77.

7 The Critics

Economic growth did not long retain the 'exalted position in the hierarchy of goals of government policy' which it achieved in western countries around 1960. A decade later, it was merely stating the obvious to point out that 'in recent years there has been an increasing tendency to doubt whether faster economic growth should be an important objective of economic policy'.[1] As a United Nations study put it,

> a quarter of a century of sustained expansion...has brought about a far more active approach to the social and physical consequences of economic growth... European governments and peoples are increasingly concerned with the effects of economic growth on the quality of the physical environment and on ways of life.[2]

This and the next two chapters describe the attacks from various quarters that came to be directed, softly in the 1950s and increasingly stridently in the 1960s, against economic growth as a policy objective. This chapter deals with social critics who questioned too exclusive preoccupation with the rate of growth of GNP, to the neglect of its composition and distribution, and emphasised the economic, social and spiritual costs of economic growth, but whose demands for reform did not, at least openly or consciously, burst the bounds of the existing social order. The next chapter will examine the contribution to the attack on economic growth made by all sorts of radical groups — ranging from the beatniks and hippies of the 'counter-culture' to the various neo-Marxist and other strands of the so-called New Left — who had in common only their rejection of the values of western society, chiefly but not only in its liberal-capitalist manifestation. Chapter nine will describe the environmentalist revolt against economic growth which reached its extreme expression in the Forrester–Meadows study, *Limits to Growth,* sponsored by the Club of Rome. Between them, these three developments in little more than a decade brought about a distinct change of perspective. How far it is overstating the case to speak of the 'fall' of economic growth as a policy objective is a question best left open until the last chapter.

After Affluence What?

The very triumph of the economic growth objective was bound to call forth dissent. To self-respecting American liberal intellectuals growthmanship was provocatively close to babbittry.

The unprecedented capacity of the post-war American economy to produce automobiles and other durables had only just begun to be demonstrated, when books such as David Riesman's *The Lonely Crowd* began to question the benefits of a consumer-oriented and conformist society.[3] By the mid-1950s concern about the social balance of the nation's production and the quality of economic growth had become a common theme in liberal intellectual circles. It found public expression when some of the most prominent in this group, including Arthur Schlesinger and J.K. Galbraith, became the brains trust and speech writers of Adlai Stevenson in his presidential campaigns of 1952 and more particularly 1956.[4]

Echoing some of the ideas put forward by Schlesinger in a programmatic essay on 'The Future of Liberalism — The Challenge of Abundance', Stevenson said in one of his speeches:

> But free society cannot be content with a goal of mere life without want... If quantity comes first so that men may eat, quality comes next so that they may not live by bread alone. Free society in the West has brought most of its citizens to that great divide. The next frontier is the quality, the moral, intellectual and esthetic standards of the free way of life.[5]

Another distinguished Harvard figure, Alvin Hansen, voiced similar disquiet:

> After ten years of almost incredible *output* performance, we need to assess not merely the speed of our growth and progress but also the direction in which we are going. What qualitative goals shall we set up? What kind of country do we wish to build? These are matters that we dare not overlook, lest we perish, as a great nation in the midst of material plenty.[6]

David Riesman asked 'Abundance for What?':

> We are coasting psychologically on the remaining gaps and
> deficiencies in the ever rising 'standard package' of consumer
> goods but, beyond that, we have very few goals, either indivi-
> dually or socially... The basic stockpile on which our society's
> dynamism has rested — the stockpile of new and exhilarating
> wants — seems to me badly depleted... No society has ever been
> in this position before, or anywhere near it... What we fear to face
> is more than total destruction: it is total meaninglessness.[7]

The manifesto which converted these questionings into slogans
that became household words throughout the western world was
Galbraith's book, *The Affluent Society*, published in 1958. Galbraith, also a Harvard economist, had some years earlier published a book which was, at least implicitly, all for growth.[8] In
American Capitalism, he had sought to explain why the American
economy, so different from the textbook model of a competitive
market economy, worked as well as it did. Accepting Schumpeter's view that monopoly is the price of technical progress under
capitalism, he had found monopoly tolerable because of the re-
gulatory function of the 'countervailing power' of organised
labour, consumers, farmers and other groups.

The Affluent Society, by contrast, was a critical and — as the
author rather proudly pointed out — an angry book.[9] Its central
thesis is quickly summarised. In a world that throughout history
has been very poor, and for the most part remains so, one small
corner populated by Europeans has attained 'great and quite
unprecedented affluence'.[10] Here, and especially in the United
States, the problem of production is solved, or within sight of
solution, with rational use of available technology. But while
'increasing affluence has been undermining the sense of urgency
associated with the production of private goods,'[11] our thinking
has not been adapted to the change. For various reasons, including
the power of vested business interests, the hold on the public
mind of the 'conventional wisdom' and a belief that growth is
necessary both for full employment and as a solvent of social tensions over distribution, production continues to be treated as the
'goal of pre-eminent importance in our life' and 'Gross National
Product as a measure of achievement'.[12]

'There remains the task of justifying the resulting flow of
goods.'[13] Galbraith's answer, like Veblen's fifty years earlier, was
'want creation', the manipulation of the consumer by advertising,

which exploits and is reinforced by emulation through conspicuous consumption. 'Production creates the wants it seeks to satisfy
— by advertising and salesmanship... As a society becomes
increasingly affluent, wants are increasingly created by the process
by which they are satisfied.'[14] But advertising does not promote
demand for all goods and services equally. 'Advertising operates
exclusively, and emulation mainly, on behalf of privately produced
goods and services.'[15] For this reason, and because of the general
view that private production adds to national wealth while public
services are at best a necessary evil,[16] there is 'an inherent tendency for public services to fall behind private production'.[17] The
result is a scandalous social imbalance between our wealth in privately produced goods and crisis in the supply of public services,
between 'private opulence and public squalor'.[18]

> The Gross National Product was rising. So were retail sales. So
> was personal income. Labor productivity had also advanced. The
> cars that could not be parked were being produced at an
> expanded rate. The children, though without schools, subject in
> the playgrounds to the affectionate interest of adults with odd
> tastes, and disposed to increasingly imaginative forms of delin-
> quency, were admirably equipped with television sets. We had
> difficulty finding storage space for the great surpluses of food
> despite a national disposition to obesity. Food was grown and
> packaged under private auspices. The care and refreshment of the
> mind, in contrast with the stomach, was principally in the public
> domain. Our colleges and universities were severely overcrowded
> and underprovided, and the same was true of the mental hospi-
> tals.[19]

Not only has the attainment of affluence left many essential
public needs — in health, education, housing, transport and urban
services — unsatisfied, it has also failed to eliminate poverty. 'In
the mid fifties, by acceptable estimate, one family in thirteen in
the United States had a cash income from all sources of less than a
thousand dollars... The hard core of the very poor was declining
but not with great rapidity.'[20] 'The most certain thing about modern poverty is that it is not efficiently remedied by a general and
tolerably well-distributed advance in income'.[21]

Galbraith, besides demanding specific measures to alleviate
poverty, called for a sustained effort to redress the social balance
by a much larger allocation of resources, through progressive
income tax, to public services, especially 'investment in human

beings', education, training and scientific opportunity for individuals.[22] With the decline in the urgency of production of goods, work and efficiency have become less important.[23] For productivity as the test of public policy it is now possible and desirable to substitute other tests — 'compassion, individual happiness and well-being, the minimization of community or other social tensions'.[24]

Galbraith's book was a brilliant tract for the times. What one reviewer said of its successor, *The New Industrial State* (1967), could equally be said of *The Affluent Society*: 'He waives the scholarly conventions in favor of a rhetoric which is designed to appeal to the lay reader... There are innumerable passages in his books which make one ache with vexation at his overgeneralization, exaggeration, and stereotyping.'[25] But this is one of the weapons of the good pamphleteer, and he could not have wished for a greater impact on the general reading public. Even among the more discriminating the initial reaction was generally sympathetic. In England, for example, John Strachey proclaimed it 'a great book' and predicted 'that twenty years after its publication, *The Affluent Society* will be exercising an influence comparable, though of a very different kind, to that exercised by *The General Theory* today'.[26] H.G. Johnson, rarely a friendly critic, confessed: 'I must say that I find it extremely convincing, at least in its broad outline.'[27]

Much of the analysis of *The Affluent Society* did not survive closer scrutiny. Johnson was quick to point out that Galbraith's dismissal of production as no longer urgent implicitly assumed, even for the United States, an unchanged distribution of income, a relatively low level of social services, a limited defence effort, and limited aid to less developed countries.[28] Others pointed out that Galbraith had greatly understated the extent of poverty in the United States; that even for the well-to-do in affluent America it was an exaggeration to speak of a 'surfeit of things'; that he generalised too readily from the United States, omitting to ask himself why there were different degrees of social imbalance in different capitalist countries; that his concept of 'want creation' quite failed to allow for the extent to which all human wants are socially conditioned, even in the most primitive societies; and that he was mis-stating the problem when he presented it as a choice between quantity and quality: 'Why must we be caught up in Galbraith's exasperating habit of stating the problem in terms of either-or? One need not be opposed to a larger GNP in order to be concerned with its composition.'[29] We shall return to some of these questions in the last chapter.

Meanwhile, however, no one who read *The Affluent Society* ever thought about economic growth again in quite the same way.

Protest against Progress

In Britain, poorer and more crowded than the United States, critics of the growth objective were less worried about affluence and more worried about the costs, the external diseconomies, of economic growth.

In 1960, an English economist, E.J. Mishan, pointed out at the end of his review of a book on *The Economics of Underdevelopment*, that the editors and authors took the desirability of economic development for granted.

> It is not suggested, of course, that all economists desirous of fostering economic growth should be requested to justify their attitude. But at a time when a large number of people in the West are voicing doubts about the effects on human happiness of the machine age in which we are caught up, it would be reassuring if the editors of a volume on how to get there, or one of the writers at least, showed some awareness that, as present trends go, the thorny path to industrialisation leads, after all, only to the wasteland of Subtopia. If they believe that somehow this ignoble fate can be circumvented, we should be told about it.[30]

About the same time, another English economist, D.M. Bensusan-Butt, ended a theoretical book *On Economic Growth* by expressing such doubts in more emphatic terms:

> When an economy is largely poor and progressing but slowly, marginal wants are clearly defined, more food, more shelter, and what men go for is justifiable on simple grounds of physiological necessity. Even when the worst of poverty lies behind it is to be presumed, in a gradual evolution, that the collective wisdom of a varied community will refine the experiments of the well-to-do minorities of one generation into the sober preferences of the majority in the next... But when accumulation is rushing forward at a headlong pace...under the wild kicks of technical progress...society reels along blindly in everything that ultimately matters to the quality of its members' lives.
>
> This is not merely or mainly a question of the incompetence of the State in coping with the provision of public services in times

of rapid change and with the discrepancies between social and private product that become so blatant during industrialization, with the smoke, stench, din and ugliness of it all. There is no reason why these things should not be done better next time. It is much more that the ultimate fruits of civilization are slow growths that need a stable environment, and that the economic motive running loose in circumstances that permit or compel violent economic change must wreck this environment. Save to the extent that rapid progress may today often serve, and in the past served more often still, to relieve real poverty, there is surely not even a presumption that it also promotes the other ends of social welfare. Name a society whose economic advance delights its statisticians and you name one in which the good qualities of its earlier life are decaying and in which no new civilization has emerged. That good will come from this evil is a possibility, but the economist cannot honestly pretend to know that it is more... He need not sneer about the economic motive...as a nasty preoccupation with money-grubbing. But equally he should not belaud it as the great engine of human progress and, from a safe position at the roadside, lead the cheers which attend the juggernaut progress of Aggregate Industrial Output.[31]

These were voices in the wilderness in 1960, though they were echoed by others in the following years. E.F. Schumacher protested that 'present-day economics, while claiming to be ethically neutral, in fact, propagates a philosophy of unlimited expansionism, without any regard to the true and genuine needs of man, which are limited'.[32] T.W. Hutchison emphasised that

it is the whole life of a community which is being acted upon when policies for rapid economic growth are enacted... Different policies aimed at combining 'full' employment, price stability and more rapid economic growth, obviously have considerable effects on the whole politico-economic constitution of society, the nature and extent of freedom, and the distribution, centralization and decentralization, not only of income, but of power.[33]

Protest against blind pursuit of material progress, in the tradition of John Stuart Mill, found its fullest expression in E.J. Mishan's book, *The Costs of Economic Growth*, published in 1967. The book was an urgent plea to the thoughtful to ponder 'the effects on the welfare of ordinary people of a gathering eruption of science and technology in pressure sufficient to splinter the framework of our institutions and to erode the moral foundations on which they have been raised'.[34] Mishan asked his readers to inspect

the blessings heaped on mankind as a result of rapid economic growth — a growing assortment of automobiles, television sets, vacuum cleaners, refrigerators, washing machines, electric tooth brushes and other anti-drudge devices, also increased air travel, antibiotics, pesticides, and reduced infant mortality

and to 'wonder whether it is really worth it; whether economic progress over the last couple of centuries has succeeded only in making life increasingly complex, frantic and wearing'.[35]

'One may concede the importance of economic growth in an indigent society, in a country with an outsize population wherein the mass of people struggle for bare subsistence.' But 'it is palpably absurd to continue talking, and acting, as if our survival — or our "economic health" — depended upon that extra one or two per cent growth'.[36] Much of the book consisted of a furious indictment of 'the less laudable consequences of economic growth over the last twenty years', the 'rapid spread of disamenities that now beset the daily lives of ordinary people'.[37] Mishan vented his particular spleen against the motor car — 'the invention of the private automobile is one of the great disasters to have befallen the human race'.[38] 'Lorries, motor-cycles and taxis belching fumes, filth and stench, snarling engines and unabating visual disturbance have compounded to make movement through the city an ordeal for the pedestrian at the same time as the mutual strangulation of the traffic makes it a purgatory for motorists.'[39] Then there are the

other disagreeable features...such as the post-war 'development' blight, the erosion of the countryside, the 'uglification' of coastal towns, the pollution of their air and of rivers with chemical wastes...and visible to all who have eyes to see, a rich heritage of natural beauty being wantonly and systematically destroyed.[40]

High up on his list of *bêtes noires* stood air travel and mass tourism which have caused 'something of a holocaust of the scarcest of our earthly resources, natural beauty' and have 'transformed once-famous resorts, Rapallo, Capri, Alassio and scores of others...into so many vulgar Coney Islands'.[41] If 'an international ban against all air travel' is too drastic a remedy, the least that should be done is to declare 'a wide selection of mountain, lake and coastal resorts and islands scattered about the globe' out of bounds for air travel and all motorised traffic.[42] He quoted drugs as an illustration of the fact that 'in many circumstances some measures of constraint on a man's choice can increase his welfare. If, for example, television or cinema audiences were deprived for a longish period of the shallow entertainment they have habitually succumbed to, many of them...might develop a taste for more sophisticated programmes'.[43]

More far-reaching in their implications were Mishan's 'More Intimate Reflections on the Unmeasurable Consequences of Economic Growth'.[44] Among these were

> the latent antagonisms between the demands of an advanced technological civilization and the demands of man's instinctual nature...a sense of intimately belonging, of being part of a community in which each man had his place; a sense of being close to nature, of being close to the soil and to the beasts of the field that served him; a sense of being part of the eternal and unhurried rhythm of life;[45]

the anxiety caused to 'every one of us, manager, workman or scientist', by the growing menace of obsolescence;[46] the 'tolerance...borne less of enlightenment as of uncertainty and bewilderment' which is fostered by television and which serves 'further to weaken the moral props of an already disintegrating society and to destroy a belief in divinity that once gave hope and comfort to many';[47] the 'loss of aesthetic and instinctual gratification suffered by ordinary working men over two centuries of technological innovation',[48] and of the 'open, easy and full-hearted relationship with one's fellows...a quality nurtured in the small agrarian society based on mutual dependence, and one of the first casualties in any society whose energies are drawn into the competitive scramble for material ends';[49] and behind it all, propelling the 'sustained technological advance which tends inexorably to destroy the sources of satisfaction of ordinary people',[50] Science — without social conscience or social purpose:

> Like some ponderous multi-purpose robot that is powered by its own insatiable curiosity, science lurches onward irresistibly, its myriad feelers peeling away the flesh of nature, probing ever deeper beneath the surface of things, forcing entry into every sanctuary, moving a transmuted humanity forward to the day when every throb in the universe has been charted, every manifestation of life dissected to the nth particle, and nothing more remains to be discovered — except, perhaps, the road back.[51]

The general conclusion of this volume is that the continued pursuit of economic growth by Western Societies is more likely on balance to reduce rather than increase social welfare... If men are concerned primarily with human welfare, and not primarily with productivity conceived as a good in itself, they should reject economic growth as a prior aim of policy in favour of a policy of seeking to apply more selective criteria of welfare,

including 'a substantial diversion of investible resources from industry to the task of re-planning our towns and cities' and 'an extension to existing minorities of separate facilities...especially in respect of viable areas wherein a man of moderate means may choose to dwell unmolested by those particular features of modern technology that most disturb his equanimity'.[52]

Mishan's was a splendidly written book which, despite the quirks and idiosyncrasies, made a mark because it painted in vivid colours costs of economic growth which were increasingly being felt by many besides the 'man of moderate means' who seeks periodic refuge from the bustle of London or Manchester in Rapallo, Capri or Alassio.

Critique of Growthmanship

Before and after the major onslaughts by Galbraith and Mishan, a growing number of critics — economists, other social scientists and philosophers — chipped away at the pretensions of the more fervent advocates of economic growth.

As early as 1955, in the first full-fledged discussion of the growth objective among British economists, H.G. Johnson declared flatly: 'Philosophically speaking, there is nothing inherently desirable in a high rate of economic growth: insistence on it as the sole criterion of efficiency for economic systems is a currently fashionable value-judgment less defensible than those economists usually make, amounting in extreme cases to pure fetishism.'[53] A few years later, Colin Clark, in a pamphlet primarily designed to urge higher priority for control of inflation even at some sacrifice of growth, and to question the importance still being attached, under the influence of the Harrod-Domar theory, to fixed capital formation as a factor in economic growth, dissociated himself from the current fashion by borrowing, for the title, Nixon's word *Growthmanship*.[54]

At the 1963 Annual Meeting of the American Economic Association, James Tobin said:

Growth has become a good word. And the better a word becomes, the more it is invoked to bless a variety of causes and the more it loses specific meaning... Let growth be something it is possible to oppose as well as to favor, depending on judgments of social priorities and opportunities.[55]

A year later, Edward Mason, in an essay on 'Objectives of a Mature Society', stressed that 'there are aspects of living that are not taken into account in the statistics of economic growth. It is quite possible for per capita incomes to increase steadily while the standard of living, in any proper sense of the term, declines'.[56] In England, Hutchison, commenting on the objective of economic growth, similarly castigated 'the crudities of its conventional measurement in terms of GNP, and the philistinism of its advocacy without taking full account of these crudities'.[57] He also thought it 'extremely uncertain how far a democratic electorate, of the current British age structure, would support the more intensive pursuit of the economic growth objective, if the essentials of the issue were plainly put to it'.[58] Too often growth, or faster growth, was being advocated without counting the cost. 'A more rapid rate of growth seemed often to be presented as something largely painlessly and costlessly super-imposable, without affecting the attainment of other equally preciously-held objectives.'[59] As another commentator put it:

The desire to avoid or blur the unpleasant choices at the margin between different priorities among policy aims, and between groups differentially affected by different policy combinations, is one reason for the popularity that faster economic growth as an explicit policy objective has acquired in some political circles in recent years.[60]

Philosophers began to write about economic growth as a policy objective, and it is not surprising that they tended to be even more unsympathetic to growthmanship. One, writing in the American journal, *Ethics*, on 'Economic Growth versus Existential Balance', amidst a good deal of confusion between wealth and income, need and demand and other economic concepts, and after a delightful illustration of the fact that people 'may be surfeited with goods' — 'less than fifty years ago a person could reach the economic goals of his life when he married, bought and furnished a house, educated his children, and accumulated some savings for his old age' while today he is 'lured further and further from rest and satisfaction by more and more new goods and gadgets' — he makes the point that

> our overemphasis on economic growth...leads to a disturbance of the balance of our existence. Too much time and energy used for the procurement of goods and services...lead to a neglect of...higher needs...the need for love and belongingness, the need for self-actualization in work...the opportunity for meaningful political action by individuals; and the dimension of contemplation in the broadest sense.[61]

At the end of the decade, John Passmore took a much more radical position still:

> The conventional 'left' and the conventional 'right' are still squabbling about who is to get what, and by what means; the Soviet Union and the United States are equally committed to the fetish of economic growth. That is one major reason why the conventional divisions between political parties now seem to many people quite irrelevant: the basic conflict, only gradually emerging, is between those who are still wholly committed to the ideal of economic growth and those who are uninterested in economic growth, except where there is clear evidence that — as it sometimes has done, and in many countries still could do — it improves the quality of men's lives, diminishes mutual suspicion, enables men to devote themselves more freely to their loves, offers them opportunities for creative enterprise, or, in short, does what the Enlightenment hoped it would do.[62]

Growth and Development

Before concluding this chapter, reference should be made briefly to another factor which, tangentially, probably contributed to a more questioning attitude to economic growth as a policy objective in the advanced countries. This was the strong reaction towards the end of the 1960s against economic growth as the primary criterion of development strategy in less developed countries.

In 1960, the United Nations declared the 1960s the First Development Decade and set as the central objective a 5 per cent annual growth of GNP in the less developed countries. In 1970, Robert McNamara, President of the World Bank, in one of several calls for a new approach to development, said:

Growth rates of GNP are entirely valid and necessary economic indicators, but they are not adequate measures of the development of a nation. Nor are they satisfactory terms in which to frame the objectives of development programs. In the First Development Decade, the primary development objective, a 5 per cent annual growth in GNP, was achieved. This was a major accomplishment. The 5 per cent rate exceeded the average growth rates of the advanced countries during their own early stages of progress in the last century. But this relatively high rate of growth in GNP did not bring satisfactory progress in development. In the developing countries, at the end of the decade: Malnutrition is common... Infant mortality is high... Life expectancy is low... Illiteracy is widespread... Unemployment is endemic and growing... The distribution of income and wealth is severely skewed... The lesson to be learned is that in setting the objectives, planning the programs, and measuring the progress of development in the Seventies, we must look to more than gross measures of economic growth.[63]

The notion that a development strategy can be formulated in terms of a target GNP growth rate was never much more than a piece of United Nations rhetoric. Even within the United Nations, at least within the Secretariat, and even at the beginning of the decade, more sophisticated views were held. A United Nations report on *The UN Development Decade: Proposals for Action* (1962) expounded as the basic thesis: 'The problem of the under-developed countries is not just growth, but development. Development is growth *plus* change; change, in turn, is social and cultural as well as economic, and qualitative as well as quantitative... The key concept must be improved quality of people's life.'[64] But it is true that well into the 1960s, in most developing countries, local policy makers and their foreign advisers concentrated on measures to expand the overall productive capacity of the economy and assumed too readily that employment would thereby be generated, poverty reduced and social conditions improved.

By the end of the decade a crusade — associated chiefly with the names of Dudley Seers and H.W. Singer at the Sussex Institute of Development Studies, and of David Morse, Director-General of the International Labour Office — for a development strategy aimed at employment and other social objectives, rather than at economic growth, had substantially won the day among those who had not altogether given up hope for peaceful change. The essence of the new doctrine, as formulated by Seers, was:

> The need is not, as is generally imagined, to accelerate economic growth — which could even be dangerous — but to change the nature of the development process... The questions to ask about a country's development are... What has been happening to poverty? What has been happening to unemployment? What has been happening to inequality? If all three of these have declined from high levels, then beyond doubt this has been a period of development for the country concerned. If one or two of these central problems have been growing worse, especially if all three have, it would be strange to call the result 'development', even if per capita income doubled.[65]

David Morse summed up 'the nature of the challenge that will face development planners in the future' in the phrase 'dethronement of the gross national product'.[66]

There were sceptics about the new approach.

> Fashions in development studies change with a rhythm that does not vary much from year to year... Indeed, they usually last for exactly a year, for the principal creators of fashion are the development agencies, national and international, seeking a 'new challenge' with which to invigorate the annual meetings which take place in Washington and elsewhere from October onwards.

'Dethronement of GNP' was 'an over-dramatisation of what was in fact a limited, but still significant, modification of previous objectives'.

> Employment creation was only one aspect of the wider objective of relieving poverty, which in turn was one aspect of the whole process of development... There was at least a *prima facie* case for supposing that growth was a necessary condition of the attainment of development objectives, including employment creation, since it was growth that provided the additional resources with which to effect changes in the structure of the economy.[67]

Nevertheless, there can be little doubt that criticism of 'mere growth' as a policy objective in less developed countries rubbed off on thinking in the advanced countries and did something to strengthen the critics.

References

1 W. Beckerman, 'The Desirability of Economic Growth', in N. Kaldor (ed.), *Conflicts of Policy Objectives* (Blackwell, Oxford, 1971), p. 38.

2 United Nations Economic Commission for Europe, *Economic Survey of Europe 1971: The European Economy from the 1950s to the 1970s* (New York, 1972), pp. 113, 119.

3 David Riesman, *The Lonely Crowd* (Yale University Press, New Haven, 1950).

. 4 B. Cochran, *Adlai Stevenson: Patrician among the Politicians* (Funk & Wagnalls, New York, 1967), p. 211.

5 Quoted in C.H. Hession and H. Sardy, *Ascent to Affluence: A History of American Economic Development* (Allyn & Bacon, Boston, 1969), p. 845.

6 A.H. Hansen, *The American Economy* (McGraw Hill, New York, 1957), p. 146.

7 David Riesman, *Abundance for What?* (Chatto & Windus, London, 1964), pp. 299–303.

8 J.K. Galbraith, *American Capitalism* (Hamish Hamilton, London, 1952).

9 J.K. Galbraith, *The Affluent Society* (Hamish Hamilton, London, 1958; Penguin, London, 1962), p. 15.

10 *Ibid.*, p. 13.

11 *Ibid.,* p. 10

12 *Ibid.*, p. 107.

13 *Ibid.*, p. 121.

14 *Ibid.*, p. 132.

15 *Ibid.*, p. 213.

16 *Ibid.*, p. 116.

17 *Ibid.*, p. 214.

18 *Ibid.*, p. 211.

19 *Ibid.*, p. 207.

20 *Ibid.*, p. 261.

21 *Ibid.*, p. 264.

22 *Ibid.*, p. 221.

23 *Ibid.*, pp. 232, 269.

24 *Ibid.*, p. 234.

25 Scott Gordon, 'The Close of the Galbraithian System', *Journal of Political Economy*, July–August 1968, p. 635.

26 John Strachey, 'Unconventional Wisdom', *Encounter*, October 1958, p. 80.

27 H.G. Johnson, 'The Political Economy of Opulence' (1960), in H.G. Johnson, *Money, Trade and Economic Growth* (Allen & Unwin, London, 1962), p. 166.

28 *Ibid.*

29 Myron E. Sharpe, *J.K. Galbraith and the Lower Economics* (International Arts and Sciences Press, White Plains, New York, 1973), p. 40; see also Gordon, *op. cit.*

30 E.J. Mishan, Review of Agarwala and Singh, *Economica*, May 1960, p. 194.

31 D.M. Bensusan-Butt, *On Economic Growth* (Clarendon Press, Oxford, 1960), pp. 212–14.

32 E.F. Schumacher, *Roots of Economic Growth* (Gandhian Institute of Studies, Varanasi, 1962), p. 13.

33 T.W. Hutchison, *'Positive' Economics and Policy Objectives* (Allen & Unwin, London, 1964), p. 154.

34 E.J. Mishan, *The Costs of Economic Growth* (Staples, London, 1967), p. xvii.

35 *Ibid.*, p.x.

36 *Ibid.*, p. 5.

37 *Ibid.*

38 *Ibid.*, p. 173.

39 *Ibid.*, pp. 5–6.

40 *Ibid.*, pp. 6–7.

41 *Ibid.*, pp. 104–5.

42 *Ibid.*, p. 106.

43 *Ibid.*, pp. 118–19.

44 *Ibid.*, p. 138.

45 *Ibid.*, pp. 123–4.

46 *Ibid.*, p. 129.

47 *Ibid.*, p. 132.

48 *Ibid.*, p. 160.

49 *Ibid.*, p. 163.

50 *Ibid.*, p. 148.

51 *Ibid.*, p. 144.

52 *Ibid.*, pp. 174–5.

53 H.G. Johnson, 'Economic Expansion and the Balance of Payments', *Bulletin*, Oxford Institute of Statistics, February 1955, p. 8.

54 Colin Clark, *Growthmanship* (Hobart Papers No. 10, Institute of Economic Affairs, 2nd edn, London, 1962).

55 James Tobin, 'Economic Growth as an Objective of Government Policy', *AEA Proceedings,* May 1964, p. 1.

56 E.S. Mason, 'Objectives of a Mature Society', in E.A. Edwards (ed.), *The Nation's Economic Objectives* (Chicago University Press, Chicago, 1964), p. 6.

57 T.W. Hutchison, *Economics and Economic Policy in Britain, 1946–66* (Allen & Unwin, London, 1968), p. 247.

58 *Ibid.*

59 *Ibid.*, p. 207.

60 Donald Winch, *Economics and Policy* (Hodder & Stoughton, London, 1969), p. 318.

61 W.A. Weisskopf, 'Economic Growth versus Existential Balance', *Ethics*, January 1965, p. 84.

62 John Passmore, *The Perfectibility of Man* (Duckworth, London, 1970), p. 321.

63 Robert S. McNamara, 'The True Dimension of the Task', *International Development Review*, 1970, vol. 1, pp. 5–6.

64 United Nations, *The UN Development Decade: Proposals for Action* (New York, 1962), p. 5.

65 Dudley Seers, 'The Meaning of Development', *International Development Review*, December 1969, p. 3.

66 David Morse, 'The Employment Problem in Developing Countries', in R. Robinson and P. Johnston (eds), *Prospects for Employment Opportunities in the Nineteen Seventies* (Cambridge University Overseas Study Committee, HMSO, London, 1971), p. 7.

67 John White, 'Economic Planning for Employment', in Robinson and Johnston, *op. cit.*, pp. 14 ff.

8 The Revolutionaries

The 1960s were the decade of the New Left. Beginning with the beatnik and hippie movements of the mid-1950s, young people dropped out, protested, demonstrated, sat-in and at times fought against racial discrimination, against nuclear tests, against the Vietnam War, against capitalism, imperialism and consumerism. There were moments during the student revolt of 1966 to 1968 when it seemed possible that governments, if not the social order, would be overturned. Out of the turmoil came new variants of Marxist and other revolutionary socialist rhetoric and thought. By 1970, the student revolt had died down and the New Left was, at least for the time being, a spent force. But a whole generation had been exposed to an intellectual and moral critique of material progress, economic growth and affluence.

Marxist Orthodoxy

How much the ideology of the extreme left in western countries changed during the 1960s is most strikingly demonstrated by recalling what was still Old Left orthodoxy in the late 1950s.

In 1957, the American Marxist economist, Paul Baran, published *The Political Economy of Growth*, for many years the standard work in the field.[1] Its critique of capitalism and advocacy of socialism differed from those expounded by Marxist writers twenty or fifty years earlier only in its explicit promise to the less developed countries and in its post-Keynesian touches. 'A socialist society in the advanced countries...would not only attack head-on the waste, irrationality, and cultural and moral degradation of the West, it would also throw its weight into helping to solve the entire problem of want, disease and starvation in the under-

101

developed parts of the world'.[2] One source of the waste and irrationality of capitalism was its inherent tendency towards underemployment, due to 'the insufficiency of investment under monopolistic capitalism',[3] proved by Keynes. 'Incapable of pursuing a policy of genuine full employment...it has to rely in the main on military spending for the preservation of the prosperity and high employment on which it depends for profits and for popular support.'[4]

An even more fundamental defect of capitalism was 'the incompatibility of sustained economic growth with the capitalist system'.[5] 'Marx and Engels considered the capitalist order itself as likely to survive only as long as it did not become a fetter on further economic and social progress.'[6] 'Behind some recent writings on problems of economic growth' — the reference is to Domar–Harrod and probably to the stagnation thesis — 'lurks a gnawing uncertainty about the future of capitalism and a painful awareness that the impediments to economic progress that are inherent in the capitalist system are bound to reappear with renewed force and increased obstinacy as soon as the extraordinary hothouse situation of the postwar period has ceased to exist.'[7]

Reform of capitalism is a forlorn hope, and the 'Keynesian Revolution' a misnomer. 'The "Keynesian Revolution" has never been associated with a vigorous movement for the abolition of an outlived and destructive social order.'[8] Liberal reformers fail to appreciate the 'desperate urgency [of]...a socialist transformation in the West' which has been accentuated by recent developments in the USSR, the denunciation of Stalinism by Khrushchev at the 20th Party Congress and the occupation of Hungary by the Soviet army.[9] 'As a result of these developments, the issue of economic and social progress...relates to the very essence of the widening and sharpening struggle between the two antagonistic social orders.'[10] Just as 'the logic of economic growth is such that a slow and gradual improvement of living standards in little-developed countries is an extremely difficult if not altogether impossible project,'[11] so 'the irrationalities of monopoly capitalism and imperialism...block economic development in advanced capitalist countries'.[12] Baran, it will be noted, made no fine distinctions between 'growth' and 'development', nor was he unduly troubled by the difficulties of measuring economic growth.

Let economic growth (or development) be defined as increase over time in per capita output of material goods... The difficulty of comparing outputs over time...the familiar index number problem...particularly vexing when what is considered is more or less rapid economic growth the outstanding characteristic of which is profound change not only in the magnitude but also in the composition of output... But we shall assume that increases of output over time can somehow be measured.[13]

On the socialist society that would follow the revolution Baran advanced little beyond Marx: 'The attainment of a social order in which economic and cultural growth will be possible on the basis of ever-increasing rational domination by man of the inexhaustible forces of nature.'[14] 'Drawing its energies from the immeasurable resources of free people, it will not only irrevocably conquer hunger, disease, and obscurantism, but in the very process of its victorious advance will radically recreate man's intellectual and psychic structure.'[15]

Khrushchev's condemnation of Stalin's rule and the subsequent Soviet invasion of Hungary had a far greater significance for the extreme left in western countries than Baran and most others realised at the time. As adherents of the New Left saw it later, 'these events put an end to the hegemony of Soviet Communism in the world radical movement'.[16] In the same year, 1956, 'Fidel Castro and his handful of followers landed from the *Granma* to conquer their Cuban homeland, and Martin Luther King led the successful Montgomery bus boycott'.[17] In 1958, Mao Tse Tung launched China on the Great Leap Forward; in 1959, Fidel Castro established his revolutionary regime in Cuba; and in those same years, the United States, following the defeat of the French army at Dien-Bien-Phu, became involved in Indochina. Socialist revolutionaries in the west, and in much of the Third World, increasingly looked to Mao's China, Castro's Cuba and Ho Chi Minh's Vietnam, rather than to the Soviet Union, for inspiration and example.

Meanwhile, support for both reformist and revolutionary critics of the affluent society came from a wholly unexpected source, the phenomenon of the 'counterculture' of beatniks and hippies, the forerunners of the 'cultural and moral revolt of the young'[18] of which the 'student revolution' of the mid-1960s became the most political manifestation.

The Counterculture

'The New Left grew out of the new conditions of post World War II America — the affluent society, the lonely crowd, the silent generation of the 1950s...the prophetic forerunners of the Beat Generation.'[19] For some years, liberal intellectuals had been discussing, with puzzlement and sorrow, the political apathy of the younger generation.[20] Indeed, the first negative reaction to affluence among the young was not political at all.

> When the postwar dropouts and the disaffected began to let their hair grow...their elders saw them as failures and called them beatniks... But the beatniks claimed they felt not beaten but beatific, as their experiments with mind-changing drugs liberated them from convention... The restlessness of the young found expression in the insistent beat of rock 'n roll. Now the Liverpool sound of the Beatles was added to the other strains of the music of rebellion.[21]

Jack Kerouac's *On the Road* (1957) 'sent a whole generation of young people on the highways enamoured with the state of nature and dreaming of escape from family and society'.[22] Throughout these years, as later at the great rock festivals of Woodstock in upstate New York and Altamont in California, they rejoiced in

> a euphoria, due in part, no doubt, to the nearly universal use of marijuana and other drugs, but also to a wonderful sense of togetherness... The songs were of simplicity and love and honesty and doing your own thing, in rejection not only of an older generation, but of a whole civilization.[23]

From the United States the cult spread to Europe. 'In Piccadilly Circus, around the fountain of love, hurrying London shoppers and clerks and passing American tourists may see the hippies vacantly watching the world go by. In other European capitals and even in distant Kathmandu, the drug-glazed eyes of the flower children stare at their alien elders.'[24]

Some have attributed economic causes to the hippie phenomenon. Paul Goodman, in his book *Growing Up Absurd* (1956), 'described the alienation and restlessness of American youth in part as a function of the fact that there were no longer any good jobs in the society',[25] and there may have been a grain of truth in this strange proposition as American universities and colleges began to turn out an oversupply of some kinds of graduates. More plausibly, the causes were seen in a more general malaise of western, and especially American, society.

Many have asserted their separateness by certain conventions of hair, clothing, speech... The underworld of the disturbed and the delinquent has often expressed its defiance of society by similar mannerisms... The break with the past was perhaps more apparent than real. Buddha and Jesus and Francis of Assisi were all in their way rebels against material wealth and the Establishment, and their followers were robed and barefoot. Cults of mysticism and piety have outraged the authorities in other times of social upheaval.[26]

The English left-wing economist, Joan Robinson, made the same diagnosis in her usual crisp style: 'A sure sign of crisis is the prevalence of cranks... The cranks are to be preferred to the orthodox because they see that there is a problem.'[27]

The student revolt also began non-politically. 'It began with the drop-outs. They had no thought of [revolt]... They simply left. Many bright boys and girls could not see the sense of enduring four to ten years of an academic grind just to get into the "rat race" in which they saw their parents trapped.'[28] The two developments which, more than any others, politicised the students in the United States were the civil rights movement and the Vietnam War.

The issue of racial discrimination, the plight of the largely disfranchised negroes of the American South and of black and other minorities in the ghettos of the northern cities, made a direct appeal to the consciences and idealism of white students, while the civil rights movement, led first by Martin Luther King and after his assassination by increasingly militant black leaders, taught them new protest techniques. When the student revolt erupted at Berkeley in 1964, 'one student leader, Mario Savio, who had spent the previous long hot summer in Mississippi as a civil rights volunteer, effectively applied his experience of civil disobedience and confrontation at the university'.[29]

The Vietnam War served for almost a decade as the inflammatory focus of radical activism, as it dragged on from year to year at mounting human and material cost, the human cost which the American forces inflicted on the enemy meticulously described and, for the first time in the history of war, brought — live on TV — into every American home, polarising American society between those who believed in the need to 'contain communism' and those who saw in American intervention merely the misdeeds of the 'military–industrial complex' and American imperialism, and slowly sapping the will and capacity of successive Administrations to continue the struggle. Among the students the related issue of the draft naturally aroused emotions nearly as violent as the war itself. 'Many students, hating the hypocrisies, and atrocities of the war and the universities' involvement in the war, came to hate almost as much the web of credits and academic irrelevancies which were their only protection from the draft',[30] but equally, 'the sudden decision of the Washington authorities to begin drafting (i.e. conscripting) the senior students...had a lot to do with the explosion'.[31]

From Berkeley the student revolt spread to other American campuses, to Harvard, Princeton and Columbia, and in 1968 to Berlin, Paris, London and Tokyo. When in May 1968 'French students joined the forces of this unofficial but dynamically real *new left international*'[32] they looked for a few heady days like toppling President de Gaulle, and 'in other circumstances — but with striking resemblances — Warsaw, Prague, and even East Germany...produced their own forms of New Leftism'.[33] In the United States and in western Europe, the student revolt concerned itself with issues of university reform, some long overdue. But the political impetus came, again and again, from the political left, the anti-Vietnam War campaign and increasingly all the other targets of contemporary radicalism — imperialism, racism, monopoly capitalism, inequality, injustice, poverty, alienation, urban decay, pollution, consumerism, and the values — as interpreted by the left — of affluent bourgeois society.

While the student revolt spread to many countries, and the New Left made inroads on the Old in most, the intellectual content of the New Left was overwhelmingly American, in origin and focus. One reason was, of course, that the United States was the most affluent among the affluent societies, exhibiting in most extreme form — exacerbated by the problem of racial minorities — the features against which the New Left protested. Another was that the United States was the 'imperialist' power *par excellence*, the hated protagonist in the cold and Vietnam Wars, the home of multi-national corporations. But this had the further consequence that, while American students and other radicals had to develop a critique of their own society, their contemporaries in western Europe and elsewhere were largely able to rely on the same critique of *American* society. Student, and more generally New Left, radicalism outside the United States contained a large element of anti-American nationalism and lived intellectually on borrowed American capital.

This also largely explains why the English-language literature of the New Left is almost wholly American, with few significant British contributions. In the case of Britain, however, there was another obstacle to New Left progress. As the most articulate leader of the short-lived British student revolt, the Pakistani Tariq Ali, complained in his book, 'the lack of a Marxist culture and tradition in Britain has always bedevilled the revolutionary movement'.[34] 'To deflect the revolutionary movement into some harmless channel' had been 'the job which the Fabians allocated to themselves and they were, unfortunately, quite successful in completing it. The grip of reformist ideology ensured that even the limited Marxism which developed in Britain was subject to extremes of insular opportunism'.[35]

Not all the ideas of the New Left were new.[36] Many came straight from the common stock of the socialist tradition, and from orthodox Marxism in particular. Some were absorbed during the 1960s from the liberal critics, Galbraith, Theobald and others;[37] some were borrowed, gratefully and uncritically, from the new environmentalist lobby. In so far as the New Left had a new and coherent ideology, with a content and thrust in sharp contrast to Marxist orthodoxy, it came from the writings of a Hegelian–Marxist philosopher, educated in Germany but since 1934 teaching and writing in the United States, Herbert Marcuse.

Marcuse

Of Marcuse's many books, the two which best exhibit his contributions to the ideology of the New Left are *One-Dimensional Man* (1964) and *Counterrevolution and Revolt* (1972).[38]

Marx expected that the socialist revolution would free the productive forces of technical progress from the irrational restrictions of capitalism, leading to ever rising productivity and living standards until the day when all needs could be met and true socialism established; and he predicted that the revolution would be accomplished by an alienated, impoverished proletariat. In both respects, classical Marxism has proved profoundly mistaken.

'The level of productivity which Marx projected for the construction of a socialist society has long since been attained in the technically most advanced countries, and precisely this achievement serves to sustain capitalist productive relations, to ensure popular support and to discredit the rationale of socialism.'[39] The productivity and efficiency of advanced industrial society, 'its capacity to increase and spread comforts, to turn waste into need...makes the very notion of alienation questionable. The people recognize themselves in their commodities; they find their soul in the automobile, hi-fi set, split-level home, kitchen equipment'.[40] Advanced industrial society is 'repressive precisely to the degree to which it promotes the satisfaction of needs which require continuing the rat race of catching up with one's peers and with planned obsolescence'.[41]

The working class, having been indoctrinated by the values of the affluent society, is no longer a possible instrument of revolution. 'The totalitarian tendencies of the one-dimensional society render the traditional ways and means of protest ineffective... "The people", previously the ferment of social change, have "moved up" to become the ferment of social cohesion.'[42] If there is to be a revolution, its agents will have to be found elsewhere.

> Underneath the conservative popular base is the substratum of outcasts and outsiders, the exploited and persecuted of other races and other colors, the unemployed and the unemployable. They exist outside the democratic process... Thus their opposition is revolutionary even if their consciousness is not... Their force is behind every political demonstration for victims of law and order. The fact that they start refusing to play the game may be the fact which marks the beginning of the end of a period.[43]

As Marcuse put it more succinctly in the later book, 'the radical goals as well as the radical strategy are confined to small minoritarian groups, middle class rather than proletarian in their composition; while a large part of the working class has become a class of the bourgeois society'.[44]

There was also a good deal about 'manipulation' and about 'true' and 'false' needs, Galbraith in Hegelian garb,[45] and a little about 'global destruction of resources, of nature, of human life', echoing the new environmentalism.[46] But the originality of Marcuse lay in his clear perception that the affluent society had the support of the great majority, including most blue collar workers, and that it was 'repression' through affluence that stood in the way of revolution or, as he put it, 'contained liberation'.[47]

Marcuse frequently described the class enemy in orthodox Marxist terms — 'vested interests',[48] 'monopoly capitalism', 'a small parasitic ruling class'[49] — and particularly in his later books resorted to increasingly intemperate language in his denunciation of the 'power structure' of the 'welfare and warfare state',[50] and of American neo-imperialism which conducts 'wholesale massacres' all over the world while, 'by the hundreds, students are slaughtered, gassed, bombed, kept in jail' at home.[51] But his real personal detestation was directed at affluence itself, the 'wasteful and enslaving conveniences of the capitalist consumer society'.[52]

If higher living standards were the obstacle to revolution, what was to be its purpose? Much of the time, Marcuse defined it in Hegelian jargon: 'pacification of existence', 'liberation', 'Reason as freedom', socialism as a 'qualitatively different *totality*'.[53] Some idea of his vision of 'the socialist universe [as] a moral and aesthetic universe'[54] is conveyed by the following passage in *Counter-revolution and Revolt*:

> What is at stake in the socialist revolution is not merely the extension of satisfaction within the existing universe of needs, nor the shift of satisfaction from one (lower) level to a higher one, but the rupture with this universe, the *qualitative leap*. The revolution involves a radical transformation of the needs and aspirations themselves, cultural as well as material; of consciousness and sensibility; of the work process as well as leisure. This transformation appears in the fight against the fragmentation of work, the necessity and productivity of stupid performances and stupid merchandise, against the acquisitive bourgeois individual, against servitude in the guise of technology, deprivation in the guise of the good life, against pollution as a way of life. Moral and aesthetic needs become basic, vital needs and drive toward new relationships between the sexes, between the generations, between men and women and nature. Freedom is understood as rooted in the fulfillment of these needs, which are sensuous, ethical, and rational in one.[55]

One need not wonder that so sublime an amalgam of the good, the beautiful and the true, of Rousseau and Marx and Freud, appealed to the young.

Here and there, Marcuse was more concrete and specific. The 'new modes of realization' to be attained by socialist revolution would include 'freedom *from* the economy — freedom from being controlled by economic forces and relationships; freedom from the daily struggle for existence, from earning a living... Intellectual freedom would mean the restoration of individual thought now absorbed by mass communication and indoctrination, abolition of "public opinion" together with its makers'.[56] 'The mere absence of all advertising and of all indoctrinating media of information and entertainment would plunge the individual into a traumatic void where he would have the chance to wonder and think.'[57] When Marcuse protests against contemporary western society for having 'invaded the inner space of privacy and practically eliminated the possibility of that isolation in which the individual, thrown back on himself, can think and question and find',[58] when he rails against 'togetherness' and 'the tyranny of the majority',[59] when he complains that 'personal withdrawal of mental and physical energy from socially required activities and attitudes is today possible only for a few',[60] when he declares that 'the standard of living attained in the most advanced and industrial areas is not a suitable model of development' and that 'in view of what this standard has made of Man and Nature, the question must again be asked whether it is worth the sacrifices and the victims made in its defense',[61] then Marcuse, the revolutionary unhappy intellectual, does not sound so very different from Mishan, the conservative unhappy intellectual.

Radical Economics

What was new in the ideology of the New Left was very largely Galbraith, refined and radicalised by Marcuse, and, as the 1960s wore on, an admixture of environmentalism. Most of the New Left thinking relevant to our theme is to be found in the voluminous literature of Radical Economics, the writings of more or less professional economists with New Left leanings.[62]

Much of radical economics consisted of criticism of conventional academic economics, its failure to concern itself with the problems that matter — 'imperialism, inequality, alienation, racism, etc.' — and to highlight the fact that they all 'directly involve economic conflicts'.[63]

> It is these pervasive relations of domination and servitude, these relations of power and authority, that lead to conflict, disharmony, and disruptive change. A political economist sees these power structures and puts them in the forefront of his analysis; a conventional economist...does not...because he sees harmonies of interest almost everywhere.[64]

'The political economist turned radical...actively takes the side of the poor and the powerless, and he generally sees the system of capitalism as their oppressor...a system that maltreats large numbers of people.'[65]

Part of the indictment against conventional economists was their 'assumption that the source of human welfare is commodities, i.e. GNP. In these terms, greater welfare requires more "productive" workers — workers molded by capitalist institutions to the narrow pursuit of producing ever more to consume ever more... *The* economic goal is growth — and that's that'.[66] Not only is such a goal limited and unworthy, it is also becoming increasingly pointless. 'In the United States today the means already exist for overcoming poverty, for supplying everyone with the necessities and conveniences of life, for giving to all a genuinely rounded education and the free time to develop their faculties to the full.'[67]

At this point, the argument naturally followed Galbraith, if not always Marcuse. 'It is important to answer Galbraith, Theobald and others who ask if this scarcity is not itself manufactured by industry and advertising in the quest for consumerism.'[68]

> While the growth of the service sector has partially compensated for the job-destroying effects of modern technology, it and related developments have added a new dimension to the dehumanization of the labor process under capitalism... A large and growing part of the product of monopoly capitalist society is, judged by genuine human needs, useless, wasteful or positively destructive.

This applies not only to the 'military machine the only purpose of which is to keep people of the world from solving their problems in the only way they can be solved, through revolutionary socialism' but also to 'many millions of other workers who produce, and create wants for, goods and services which no one needs'.[69] But whereas Galbraith called for a better social balance and other reforms of the existing system — and was duly flayed by the radicals as an apologist for capitalism[70] — radical economists concluded that 'we have reached a point where the only true rationality lies in action to overthrow what has become a hopelessly irrational system'.[71]

Sometimes the revolution was still described in the simple terms of traditional revolutionary socialism —'expropriation of the capitalist class and the turning over of ownership of capital goods and land to all the people'.[72] But the lesson of Soviet experience had begun to be learned. 'Even if the State "takes over" the economy and equalizes wages, the whole system may be condemned if man becomes a slave to a new bureaucracy.'[73] In fact, it was generally true that 'the radical movement...repudiates the Stalinist bureaucracy of the Soviet Union'.[74] As in the New Left in general, there was among radical economists 'increasing partiality to China and Cuba'.[75] For Fidel Castro 'communism must mean abundance without egoism'[76] and 'Mao Tse Tung conceived of a revolution that would really be in the interests of the people'.[77] As one, generally sympathetic, critic described this aspect of radical economics, 'the hope seems to be that cultural revolution and the "mass line" of the Chinese, plus Cuban "Marxist humanism", can somehow be compounded in a dialectic synthesis, with the merits of both Yugoslavia and the Gosplan but with the faults of neither. To an outsider like the present writer', he added, 'this seems a matter of blind faith, approaching Tertullian's *credo quia absurdum*.'[78]

Baran and Sweezy, in their joint work, *Monopoly Capitalism* (1966), accepted Marcuse's diagnosis that the revolution, if it comes, will have to be accomplished by the special victims of contemporary capitalism, 'unemployed and unemployables, migrant farm workers, school dropouts', not by the industrial proletariat which has been 'integrated into the system as consumers and ideologically conditioned members of the society'.[79] But they were not optimistic that these groups, 'too heterogeneous, too scattered and fragmented', would be equal to the task.[80] Instead, like most radicals in the west towards the end of the 1960s, they placed their hopes on 'the revolutionary peoples [who already] have achieved a series of historic victories in Vietnam, China, Korea, Cuba and Algeria'.[81]

Since most radical economists saw in monopoly capitalism the root of all evil — not merely of militarism, imperialism, racism, poverty, inequality, and the subjugation of women, but even of 'the emptiness and purposelessness of life in capitalist society [which] stifles the desire to do anything', of mindless TV programmes and 'unimaginable brutality to children', of the 'degeneration of conversation into chatter', the fact that 'social gatherings are motivated...by fear of being alone' and the 'grinding, debilitating boredom' which is produced as much by leisure as by work[82] — they tended to assume, explicitly or implicitly, that these evils would disappear under socialism. 'For behind the emptiness, the degradation, and the suffering which poison human existence in this society lie the profound irrationality and moral bankruptcy of monopoly capitalism itself.'[83] As one young radical economist blithely explained: A conventional economist like Peter Wiles is hopelessly utopian, in the pejorative sense of that term, because he believes that perverse institutions can somehow create 'good' societies... Socialist thought is grounded in the belief that if the pernicious institutions that have hitherto governed men are destroyed and replaced by others compatible with man's basic needs, no limits can be placed on the possibilities of mankind.[84]

But what are man's basic needs? To most radicals, utopia was no longer the 'economy of abundance' — 'with all goods free and all labor voluntary'[85] — although some out-Galbraithed Galbraith by claiming that 'our productive resources are such that people could live without working' and that it is only capitalism that 'requires that people work in order to live'.[86] Not all radicals followed Marcuse in his demand for 'reduction' of the 'over-development' of advanced industrial countries to 'a new [lower] standard of living'[87] but many were attracted by his vision of 'liberation'. In the glowing words of a young disciple: 'A new society in which men would be free from alienated labor and the restraints of repressive civilization and able to create a new culture of freedom on the basis of humane relationships and values.'[88]

Some of Marcuse's followers were perceptive enough to ask: 'What happens when the development of advanced technology brings a higher and higher rate of per capita productivity?'[89] The answer they gave would have surprised most adherents of the Old Left:

> It is not the 'riches' of the 'wealthy' which constitute the real wealth of an advanced industrial society but the enormous productive capacity of the society as a whole. The capitalist governing class is a historically reactionary force, not because it lives better lives or consumes more commodities, but because its power over society through control of the means of production prevents the realization of the historical potential which exists... The revolutionary transformation of capitalist society is not a question of 'soaking the rich'. It is rather a question of...depriving those who have power of their control over social wealth in order that we may create a free society[90]

— a conclusion which seemed to have implications for other contemporary systems besides capitalism.

In the last resort, all radical economists shared Marcuse's dilemma: 'Marx and Engels...saw the solution in the maximum development through scientific and technological advance of the productivity of human labour.'[91] 'Capitalism, in Marx's view, stood in the way of true freedom because it fettered the development of production and technology.'[92] What if Bensusan-Butt and Mishan were right in seeing, as the root cause of the evils of repressive affluent society, not capitalism but the very scientific and technological advance from which Marx expected the true freedom? To assume that, 'as the world revolution spreads...the socialist countries [will] show by their example that it is possible to use man's mastery over the forces of nature to build a rational society satisfying the human needs of human beings'[93] seemed another act of faith. Joan Robinson's answer to the same question, that 'the task of the generation now in rebellion is to reassert the authority of morality over technology',[94] was hardly more convincing.

References

1 Paul Baran, *The Political Economy of Growth* (Monthly Review Press, New York; 1957).

2 *Ibid.*, p. viii.

3 *Ibid.*, p. 87.

4 *Ibid.*, p. 129.

5 *Ibid.*, p. 11.

6 *Ibid.*, p. 5.

7 *Ibid.*, p. 9.

8 *Ibid.*, p. 8.

9 *Ibid.*, p. viii.

10 *Ibid.*, p. 10.

11 *Ibid.*, p. 13.

12 *Ibid.*, p. 17.

13 *Ibid.*, pp. 18–19.

14 *Ibid.*, p. 297.

15 *Ibid.*, p. 300.

16 Staughton Lynd, 'Towards a History of the New Left', in Priscilla Long (ed.), *The New Left* (Porter Sargent, Boston, 1969), p. 2.

17 *Ibid.*, p. 3.

18 J.B. and A.M. Bingham, *Violence and Democracy* (World Publishing Co., New York, 1970), p. 39.

19 G. Calvert and C. Neiman, *A Disrupted History: The New Left and the New Capitalism* (Random House, New York, 1971), p. 11.

20 Cf. Daniel Bell, *The End of Ideology* (Free Press, Glencoe, Illinois, 1960).

21 Bingham, *op. cit.*, p. 19.

22 Henri Avron, *Le Gauchisme* (Presses Universitaires de France, Paris, 1974), p. 83.

23 Bingham, *op. cit.*, pp. 20–1.

24 *Ibid.*, p. 22.

25 Quoted in Calvert and Neiman, *op. cit.*, p. 54.

26 Bingham, *op. cit.*, p. 17.

27 Joan Robinson, 'The Second Crisis of Economic Theory', *AEA Proceedings*, May 1972, p. 8.

28 Bingham, *op. cit.*, p. 39.

29 *Ibid.*, p. 40.

30 *Ibid.*

31 D.W. Brogan, 'The Student Revolt', *Encounter*, July 1968, p. 20.

32 Calvert and Neiman, *op. cit.*, p. 30.

33 *Ibid.*

34 Tariq Ali, *The Coming British Revolution* (Jonathan Cape, London, 1972), p. 174.

35 *Ibid.*, p. 180.

36 M. Bronfenbrenner, 'Radical Economics in America, 1970', *Journal of Economic Literature*, September 1970, p. 750.

37 See ch. 7.

38 H. Marcuse, *One-Dimensional Man* (Routledge & Kegan Paul, London, 1964) (hereafter cited as *ODM*); *Counterrevolution and Revolt* (Allen Lane, London, 1972) (hereafter cited as *C & R*); cf. also *Eros and Civilization* (Routledge & Kegan Paul, London, 1956) ('the most exciting work available to young Marxists in the early 1960's', Calvert and Nieman, *op. cit.*, p. 37); *An Essay on Liberation* (Beacon Press, Boston, 1972); *Five Lectures* (Allen Lane, London, 1970).

39 *C&R*, p. 3.

40 *ODM*, p. 9.

41 *Ibid.*, p. 241.

42 *Ibid.*, p. 256.

43 *Ibid.*, pp. 256–7.

44 *C&R*, pp. 4–5.

45 E.g., *ODM*, pp. 4, 12; *C & R*, p. 16.

46 *C&R*, p. 16.

47 *ODM*, p. 242.

48 *Ibid.*, p. 3.

49 *C&R*, p. 7.

50 *ODM*, p. 242.

51 *C&R*, p. 1.

52 *Ibid.*, p. 3.

53 *Ibid.*

54 *Ibid.*

55 *Ibid.*, pp. 15–16.

56 *ODM*, p. 4.

57 *Ibid.*, p. 245.

58 *Ibid.*, p. 244.

59 *Ibid.*, p. 242.

60 *Ibid.*, p. 243.

61 *Ibid.*, p. 242.

62 Cf., e.g., D. Mermelstein (ed.), *Economics: Mainstream Readings and Radical Critiques* (Random House, New York, 1970); E.K. Hunt and J.G. Schwartz (eds), *A Critique of Economic Theory* (Penguin, London, 1972); A Lindbeck, *The Political Economy of the New Left* (Harper, New York, 1972); Bronfenbrenner, *op. cit.*; R.C. Edwards et al., 'A Radical Approach to Economics: Basis for a New Curriculum', *AEA Proceedings*, May 1970; and extensive bibliographies in all of these.

63 Edwards, *op. cit.*, p. 353.

64 J.G. Gurley, 'The State of Political Economics', *AEA Proceedings*, May 1971, p. 55.

65 *Ibid.*

66 *Ibid.*, p. 60.

67 P. Baran and P. Sweezy, *Monopoly Capital* (Monthly Review Press, New York, 1966), p. 341.

68 M. Zweig, 'A New Left Critique of Economics', in Mermelstein, *op. cit.*, p. 26.

69 Baran and Sweezy, *op. cit.*, p. 344.

70 Cf., e.g., Bob Fitch, 'A Galbraith Reappraisal: The Ideologue as Gadfly', in Hunt and Schwartz, *op. cit.*

71 Baran and Sweezy, *op. cit.*, p. 363.

72 Gurley, *op. cit.*, p. 59.

73 J.G. Gurley, quoted in Bronfenbrenner, *op. cit.*, p. 756.

74 Mermelstein, *op. cit.*, p. 591.

75 Bronfenbrenner, *op. cit.*, p. 754.

76 Mermelstein, *op. cit.*, p. 592.

77 Joan Robinson, *Freedom and Necessity* (Allen & Unwin, London, 1970), p. 100.

78 Bronfenbrenner, *op. cit.*, p. 754.

79 Baran and Sweezy, *op. cit.*, p. 363.

80 *Ibid.*

81 *Ibid.*, p. 365; cf. also Gurley, *op. cit.*, p. 62; Marcuse, *C&R*, p. 2.

82 Baran and Sweezy, *op. cit.*, pp. 346 ff.

83 *Ibid.*, p. 363.

84 Mermelstein, *op. cit.*, p. 588.

85 Bronfenbrenner, *op. cit.*, p. 758.

86 Calvert and Neiman, *op. cit.*, p. 86.

87 Marcuse, *ODM*, pp. 242–3.
88 Calvert and Neiman, *op. cit.*, p. 103.
89 *Ibid.*, p. 95.
90 *Ibid.*, pp. 100–1.
91 Baran and Sweezy, *op. cit.*, p. 341.
92 Mermelstein, *op. cit.*, p. 593.
93 Baran and Sweezy, *op. cit.*, p. 367.
94 Joan Robinson, *Freedom and Necessity*, p. 124.

9 The Prophets

When U Thant, Secretary-General of the United Nations, launched the First Development Decade in May 1962, he contrasted the daunting problems of the less developed countries with the situation in the developed countries, as he then saw it:

> The truth, the central stupendous truth about developed economies today is that they can have — in anything but the shortest run — the kind and scale of resources they *decide* to have... It is no longer resources that limit decisions. It is the decision that makes the resources. This is the fundamental, revolutionary change — perhaps the most revolutionary mankind has ever known.[1]

In the same year, two American specialists on resource problems expressed much the same view, hardly less firmly if less dramatically:

> Recognition of the possibility of technological progress clearly cuts the ground from under the concept of Malthusian scarcity... The scientific age differs in kind, and not only in degree, from the preceding mechanical age. Not only ingenuity but, increasingly, understanding; not luck but systematic investigation, are turning the tables on nature, making her subservient to man.[2]

Ten years later such optimism was rare. There was widespread concern about the damage economic growth was doing to the environment, and influential voices were trying to persuade public opinion that the world was rapidly approaching the limits to growth set by destruction of the 'biosphere' or exhaustion of non-renewable resources or both. The prophets of doom powerfully supported the critics and the revolutionaries in their attack on economic growth as a policy objective, arguing that economic growth was not merely undesirable but, before long, impossible. This chapter will try to explain how and why economic growth came under fire from this quarter.

Conservation

Conservation as a minority concern and outlet for practical idealism had a long history, especially in the United States, long before the emergence of the new environmentalism in the 1960s. As an organised movement, it began in the United States in 1873 when fear of an impending timber famine led the American Association for the Advancement of Science to set up a committee 'to memorialize Congress and the several State legislatures upon the importance of promoting the cultivation of timber and the preservation of forests'.[3] Over the next thirty years, culminating at a Governors Conference called by President Theodore Roosevelt in 1908, fear of exhaustion of natural resources remained the predominant theme, with intermittent predictions of exhaustion within a few decades of coal, iron ore, oil and gas, phosphate and many other materials.[4]

As all such predictions were progressively falsified by events, the movement turned increasingly to other causes, especially the preservation of wild life and protection of 'the social and aesthetic values of the environment for succeeding generations'.[5] Over the years, the conservation movement did much good work, particularly through the promotion of national parks and nature reserves, although at times it seemed to merit Galbraith's jibe that 'the conservationist is a man who concerns himself with the beauties of nature in roughly inverse proportion to the number of people who can enjoy them'.[6]

In the early 1950s, the immediate demands of the Korean War and the longer-term defence implications of the cold war led to renewed anxiety in the United States about the adequacy of the nation's supplies of raw materials. President Truman set up a Materials Policy Commission (Paley Commission) which in 1952 produced a five volume report on *Resources for Freedom*.[7] While it voiced the then current concern about 'soaring demands, shrinking resources'[8] and forecast — wrongly as it turned out — a decline in the USA's terms of trade due to rising world prices of raw materials, the report in general deprecated alarmism. It expounded home truths on such popular fallacies as the notion 'that we will suddenly wake up to find the last barrel of oil exhausted or the last pound of lead gone, and that economic activity has suddenly collapsed', rather than realising that, at worst, 'we face instead the threat of having to devote constantly increasing effort to win each pound of materials from resources which are dwindling both in quantity and quality'.[9] It recommended stockpiling of strategic materials and the establishment of a mainly fact-gathering National Security Resources Board.[10]

A useful by-product of the Korean War flurry was the establishment in Washington in 1952 of 'Resources for the Future', an institute, financed by the Ford Foundation, for 'research and education in the development, conservation and use of natural resources',[11] which has since then been responsible for much valuable research and informed commentary on resource problems.

During the 1950s, following the collapse of the Korean War commodity boom, fears about materials scarcity subsided. For some years, as world production of several raw materials and foodstuffs ran ahead of demand, primary producing countries complained about low prices, and the Argentinian economist, Raul Prebisch, even formulated a 'law' concerning the inevitable secular tendency for the terms of trade to move against primary products.[12] By 1958, American conservationists had come to think that protection of the social and aesthetic values of the natural environment would 'ultimately become the objective of the movement, since increasingly the adequacy of supply of such resources as water and minerals has become a matter of economics'.[13] Two years later, a conference of economists on *Natural Resources and Economic Growth* concluded that 'as an economy progresses technologically, the role played by land and natural resources in its economic development declines'.[14] While Malthusian pressure of population on land presents grave problems in some parts of the world, 'a complex modern society (though not presumably a simple, tradition-ridden society) may respond in a variety of ways and thereby cushion the incidence of increasing scarcity'.[15]

But while confidence that resource scarcity had ceased to be a pressing problem remained generally unshaken, problems of the quality of the environment were coming to be regarded as very serious.

> More and more of the pressing problems and issues of all natural resources, not just water, are coming to be those of quality rather than quantity... Today, in the middle 1960's, many of the worries over supply have subsided. For the next generation — and probably longer — there are few indications of widespread and persistent shortages of materials. Instead, the most troublesome questions are likely to concern the cleanliness of water and air; the effects of heavy use of pesticides upon soil and water; availability of suitable surroundings for outdoor recreation; the beauty of the countryside; and the effects of urban living upon the human body and spirit.[16]

The reasons for this new emphasis were only too obvious —

pollution of air, land and water in all the highly industrialised countries.

Pollution

Modern environmentalism has its origins in Los Alamos and Hiroshima. Maddox's admirable account is worth an extensive quotation.

> The first environmentalists were probably the scientists who, toward the end of World War II, sensed that the development of nuclear weapons posed a grave threat to the human race. In 1945, Dr J. Robert Oppenheimer, the scientific director of the Los Alamos program that produced the first atomic bomb, made the point with characteristic eloquence: 'In some crude sense which no vulgarity, no overstatement can quite extinguish, the physicists have known sin, and this is a knowledge which they cannot lose.' Throughout the fifties, the campaign to ban the testing of nuclear weapons picked up momentum. In the early years of the decade, the first test explosions of hydrogen bombs carried the scientists' initial sense of alarm to a far wider spectrum of the population. In 1954, when four Japanese fishermen were killed by radioactive dust from a thermonuclear explosion, the entire world was given a vivid demonstration of the potential destructiveness of nuclear energy. By the late fifties, nuclear weapons tests had become commonplace, and the amount of radioactive fallout was reaching intolerable levels. The discovery of strontium 90 in the skeletons of young children was a powerful assault on the public conscience. With military strategy still dominated by plans for thermonuclear retaliation, it was no wonder that the decade ended with the sense that doomsday was just around the corner.

> At about the same time, ironically, the concern of the early environmentalists with the perils of nuclear explosions to human health began to win wide acceptance, and in 1963 the major powers signed a treaty prohibiting above-ground testing of nuclear weapons. Suddenly, the environmentalists constituted an army that had tasted blood but seemingly had no further battles to fight. The year before, Rachel Carson had published a now-famous study of the misuse of pesticides, *Silent Spring*, thereby launching an entirely new phase of the environmental movement. The problem was that many environmentalists continued to use the same apocalyptic rhetoric they had employed so effectively to express their indignation over the unregulated dissemination of nuclear weaponry — a truly apocalyptic danger — to describe a much more subtle and complex phenomenon.[17]

For some years before *Silent Spring*, pollution problems had made news. In the winter of 1952 smog in London was officially estimated to have been responsible for 4000 excess deaths.[18] In 1953, increasing air pollution in Los Angeles was found to be due largely to emission of hydrocarbons by automobile exhausts.[19] The discovery in Wisconsin of cranberries sprayed with a possibly carcinogenous chemical caused a furore in the American press in 1959.[20] In increasing volume in the late 1950s and early 1960s, reports came of air pollution in New York, Tokyo and other cities; of pollution by industrial waste and synthetic detergents and fertiliser of lakes, such as Lake Erie, and rivers, such as the Rhine; of problems of urban garbage disposal presented by 'non-bio-degradable' substances such as plastics; of soil erosion; of 'noise pollution'; and of spoliation of the countryside by mining operations, land development and mass tourism.

For the first time, 'ecology' became a household word, occasionally in its sober scientific definition as 'the study of the reaction of plants and animals to their immediate environment, to their habitat',[21] more often in the vivid rhetorical terms used a century earlier, in 'the first work to describe man's destructiveness',[22] G.P. Marsh's *Man and Nature*:

> The ravages committed by man subvert the relations and destroy the balance which nature had established between her organic and her inorganic creations; and she avenges herself upon the intruder, by letting loose upon her defaced provinces destructive energies hitherto kept in check by organic forces destined to be his best auxiliaries, but which he has unwisely dispersed and driven from the field of action.[23]

An enormous environmentalist literature began to pour forth, from scientific articles and monographs, official reports, textbooks, readings and handbooks to popularisations in books, magazines and newspapers.

Inevitably, the evidence of increasingly widespread and serious environmental problems was linked with economic growth. It seemed obvious that 'more output means more pollution',[24] and if the question was posed why these problems should, after two centuries of industrial development, have become so serious so suddenly, the explanation was seen partly in a greatly increased 'output of pollutants per unit of production resulting from the introduction of new productive technologies since 1946'[25] and partly in scale: 'Up to a certain level of concentration, disposal of wastes, disfigurement of the landscape, and congestion are, at worst, local irritations. Air, water, and earth-room can absorb a lot without great damage. Beyond that point real trouble ensues; differences of degree create differences of kind.'[26] In other words, the costs of economic growth are liable to rise suddenly and steeply 'when one small straw is laid on some existing back'.[27]

In the late 1960s, environmentalist protest against pollution, and against economic growth as its chief cause, assumed increasingly shrill tones. Some ecologists began to claim that some forms of pollution, especially thermal pollution, were causing irreversible changes which would sooner or later make life on earth impossible: 'Man is on a collision course with disaster if he tries to keep energy production growing by means that will impose increased thermal stress on the earth.'[28] At a popular level, this was translated into a conviction that economic growth

> in any event cannot be sustained indefinitely in view of the natural limits of the ecosystem... We are in an environmental crisis because the means by which we use the ecosphere to produce wealth are destructive of the ecosphere itself. The present system of production is self-destructive; the present course of human civilization is suicidal.[29]

Economists, while increasingly impressed by the importance and urgency of such 'external diseconomies' of economic growth,[30] tended to be less extreme in their reaction:

> Granting that most of the pressures upon the natural environment have been direct or indirect results of a prosperous and expanding economy, does it follow that further erosion of environment must continue to be the price of further economic gains? There is no pat answer. The most one can say is that continued decline does not appear inevitable. On the hopeful side are a vigorous technology and a capacity — if pressed hard enough — for political innovation and social discipline. On the other side are the difficulty and unfamiliarity of some of the present and prospective problems. Even a tolerable degree of success will not come easily.[31]

As someone said, it was no longer economics but ecology that was the 'dismal science'.

In fact, in relation to some of the more obvious problems of pollution, an aroused public opinion brought pressure on governments in all western countries which before long yielded results. Some at least of the dire predictions of the environmentalists proved to be self-refuting prophecies. This applied especially in the United States where, as a British observer has suggested, 'the peculiar virulence of the American ecological movement and its religious crusading spirit may be related to the relative failure of the American social system to establish elementary planning controls and social services of the type that have long been familiar in Europe'.[32]

Pressure by the environmentalist lobby caused Congress in 1958 to legislate on outdoor recreation resources, induced President Johnson to include an environmental plank in his 1964 'Great Society' campaign platform, and led the Nixon Administration to secure the passage in 1969 of a comprehensive *National Environmental Policy Act*.[33] The new federal Environmental Protection Agency followed up earlier legislation, such as a *Clean Air Act* (1967), a *Water Quality Control Act* (1970) and a *Resource Recovery Act* (1970), with a far-ranging programme for environmental quality control. In its fourth annual report (1973) it put forward an estimate of $275 billion for the cost of pollution abatement in the ensuing decade, or about 2.5 per cent of GNP.[34] While there was clearly a long way to go in remedying past omission, there was increasing evidence that environmental pollution, especially of the air in the major cities and of lakes and rivers was being effectively reduced.[35]

In Britain, action had begun to be taken earlier. In direct response to the public outcry provoked by the smog calamity of 1952, a *Clean Air Act* was passed in 1956 which, in little more than a decade, reduced smoke pollution in Central London by 80 per cent and increased December sunshine by 70 per cent. By 1971, 'almost all observers...agreed that East London and the industrial towns of the North [were] almost unrecognisable as a result of the successful reduction of smoke pollution from domestic and industrial sources'.[36] Similar action was taken in most western countries (and not least in Japan) to combat air and water pollution, to encourage recycling and the use of bio-degradable materials, and to promote the development of harmless substitutes for the deleterious pesticides (though premature restrictions on the use of DDT had to be reversed in several countries when insect pests threatened forests or death rates from malaria began to rise again).[37]

By the early 1970s, it had to be admitted that 'the fundamental question of whether increases in material output are necessarily linked with equal or greater increases in pollution remains unanswered'.[38] But at least it had been demonstrated that environment problems could be tackled by various

> abatement techniques which social pressure can bring into play... The problem thus appears one of implementing best technical practice, on the one hand, and of educating public behaviour, on the other. Where existing techniques and knowledge are not sufficient, a fruitful area exists for the reallocation of research and development effort towards anti-pollution, and general welfare, ends.[39]

For some time, however, such sober counsel, and even the practical achievements of anti-pollution measures, made little impression on public opinion, in the face of a new and more extreme version of the environmentalist onslaught which drew on old Malthusian as well as new ecological arguments to predict an inevitable and early end to economic growth.

Spaceship Earth

One of the first to suggest that economic growth, or at least growth of personal consumption, might have to be restrained to conserve resources was Galbraith. Speaking at a forum, organised in 1958 by Resources for the Future, on 'How Much Should a Country Consume?', he commented on the American economy's 'gargantuan and growing appetite' for resources.

> In the face of this vast use, what is happening to our domestic reserves of ores, to our energy sources, to the renewable resources?... If we are concerned about our great appetite for materials, it is plausible to seek to increase the supply, to decrease the waste, to make better use of the stocks that are available, and to develop substitutes. But what of the appetite itself? Surely this is the ultimate problem. If it continues its geometric course, will it not one day have to be restrained? Yet in the literature of the resource problem this is the forbidden question. Over it hangs a nearly total silence.[40]

He went on to criticise the Paley Commission for its 'belief that economic stagnation is the alternative to growth... Clearly we can have different rates of growth of consumption... In any case...it would obviously be better to risk stagnation now than to use up our reserves and have not stagnation but absolute contraction later'.[41] After criticising 'those who sanctify growth' and scoffing at the notion that 'uninhibited consumption has something to do with individual liberty',[42] he suggested that 'a wide range of instruments of social control' could be used to shift 'consumption patterns from those which have a high materials requirement to those which have a much lower requirement'. He gave smaller cars as one illustration and public services as another. 'Education, health services, sanitary services, good parks and playgrounds, orchestras, effective local government, a clean countryside, all have rather small materials requirements.'[43]

In making these comments and suggestions, however, Galbraith was careful to add the important qualification — 'if conservation is an issue'. On this crucial point, he was not, at that time, willing to commit himself. 'If the appetite presents no problems — if resource discovery and the technology of use and substitution promise automatically to remain abreast of consumption and at moderate cost — then we need press matters no further.'[44] One has the impression that Galbraith had found a useful further debating point in support of his arguments of *The Affluent Society* of the year before. But in substance he fully anticipated the Forrester–Meadows thesis on *The Limits to Growth*. It is intriguing that one of the discussants of Galbraith's paper anticipated the very words: 'We have never as a nation seriously considered the alternative to growth, even though I suspect there is no one who would not be forced to admit that on a finite globe...there must be some limit to "growth".'[45]

The early 1960s were the first years of space exploration, of astronauts reaching for the moon. Spaceships, translated from science fiction to the real world, offered a vivid new metaphor of which Adlai Stevenson appears to have been the first to take advantage. In his last speech as US Ambassador to the United Nations in January 1965 he warned against the danger of global nuclear conflict: 'We, the human race, are fellow travellers on a tiny space ship spinning through infinite space.'[46] A little later, Barbara Ward used *Space Ship Earth* as the title of a book in which she discussed the international power struggle, the widening gap between rich and poor countries and the conflict of ideologies.[47] To both Adlai Stevenson and Barbara Ward, the homely moral of the metaphor was: 'We are a ship's company on a small ship. Rational behaviour is the condition of survival.'[48] About the same time, the economist, Kenneth Boulding, gave the image a new interpretation which came to be very influential in the following years.[49]

In an essay on 'The Economics of the Coming Spaceship Earth', he contrasted the 'open' economy of the past with the 'closed' economy of the future. He called the former the 'cowboy' economy,

> the cowboy being symbolic of the illimitable plains and also associated with reckless, exploitative, romantic and violent · behavior, which is characteristic of open societies. The closed economy of the future might similarly be called the 'spaceman' economy, in which the earth has become a single spaceship, without unlimited reservoirs of anything, either for extraction or pollution, and in which, therefore, man must find his place in a cyclical ecological system which is capable of continuous reproduction of material form even though it cannot escape having inputs of energy.[50]

'Even the most optimistic predictions would expect the easily available supply of fossil fuels to be exhausted in a mere matter of centuries at present rates of use'; and although the economic use of energy through nuclear fusion 'would expand the time horizons...by perhaps tens to hundreds of thousands of years', the technical possibility of this source of energy could not yet be counted upon.[51] He concluded that in a spaceman economy, by contrast to the cowboy economy,

> the essential measure of success of the economy is not production and consumption at all, but the nature, extent, quality and complexity of the total capital stock... This idea that both production and consumption are bad things rather than good things is very strange to economists, who have been obsessed with the income-flow concepts.[52]

Economists, accustomed to thinking that people's living standards depend on the flow of satisfactions they derive from consumption of goods and services and unaware of any new evidence suggesting that the earth had been transformed, or was about to be transformed, from a condition of 'unlimited reservoirs' to one 'primarily concerned with...maintenance of a given total stock' of resources,[53] tended to treat Boulding's essay as a *jeu d'esprit*. But ecologists took up the idea with alacrity. They drew the inference that mankind must move, sooner rather than later, *Toward a Steady-State Economy*, where 'by "steady state" is meant a constant stock of *physical* wealth (capital), and a constant stock of people (population)... Given the size of stocks, the throughput should be minimized, since it is really a cost'.[54] Some environmentalists placed more weight on limits set to extraction, others to those set by pollution. One concluded that, while 'the classical economists thought the steady state would be made necessary by limits on the depletion side...the main limits in fact seem to be occurring on the pollution side... Air and water are used freely by all, and the result is a competitive, profligate exploitation'.[55] While economists, even Boulding, thought it was 'frequently our ignorance of the physics and chemistry of the atmosphere, or of the biology of large ecosystems, which holds us up on the practical side of environmental improvement',[56] in natural scientists — or at least in some — Boulding's Spaceship Earth message seemed to evoke a gut feeling of conviction:

> Economists must...sacrifice large intellectual (and material?) vested interests in the perpetual growth theories and policies of the last thirty years before they can really come to grips with these questions. The advantage of the physical scientists is that, unlike economists, they are viscerally convinced that the world is a finite, open system at balance in a steady state.[57]

In the last years of the decade an extremist fringe of the environmentalist movement incorporated these ideas in what critics later described as the Doomsday Syndrome.[58]

Doom

All through the 1950s and 1960s, a recurrent theme in discussion of the problems of the less developed countries was concern that, in some of the most densely populated areas, pressure of population on the available land would give rise to Malthusian crises of malnutrition and famine and that, more generally, the acceleration of population growth that was resulting from declining mortality rates would frustrate efforts to raise per capita income. It was this theme which one of the most vocal and influential of the American prophets of doom, Paul Ehrlich, picked up in his first popular book, *The Population Bomb* (1968).[59] Arguing that not merely some parts of the less developed world, but the whole world, was already overpopulated, he advocated the most determined efforts in all countries, developed and developing alike, to achieve zero population growth as soon as possible.

A year later, he expanded this theme into a full-fledged prophecy of 'Eco-Catastrophe':[60]

The end of the ocean came late in the summer of 1979... There had been the final gasp of the whaling industry in 1973, and the end of the Peruvian anchovy fishery in 1975... By 1977 the annual yield of fish from the sea was down to...less than one-half of the per capita catch a decade earlier...It became apparent in the early 1970s that the 'Green Revolution' was more talk than substance... At home, in the USA the early '70s were traumatic times... Community after community was forced to close its schools...for lack of funds... Water rationing occurred in 1,723 municipalities in the summer of 1974, and hepatitis and epidemic dysentery rates climbed about 500 per cent between 1970 and 1974... Air pollution continues to be the most obvious manifestation of environmental deterioration. It was, by 1972, quite literally in the eyes of all Americans... Deaths in the late 1960s caused by smog were well known to scientists...but suddenly citizens were faced with nearly 200,000 corpses... The population was terrorized as TV screens became filled with scenes of horror from the disaster areas... By September 1979 all important animal life in the sea was extinct...Japan and China...faced with almost instant starvation from a total loss of seafood...blamed Russia for the situation... On October 13, Chinese armies attacked Russia on a broad front.

So much for the prophecy. To drive the lesson home, the author reminded his readers that 'more than three and a half billion people already populate our moribund globe, and about half of them are hungry. Some 10 to 20 million will starve to death *this year* [1969]'. And so forth.[61]

Perhaps it is not fair to unearth these prophecies when enough time has elapsed to demonstrate their absurdity (though for that very reason prophets do well to prophesy a hundred rather than five years ahead). Perhaps also Ehrlich did not mean this particular piece to be taken too seriously, though it was enthusiastically reprinted in the following year in *The Environmental Handbook*, prepared for the First National Environmental Teach-In and published in a 'Friends of the Earth Book' series which also contained *The Frail Sun, S/S/T and Sonic Boom Handbook*, and *Perils of the Peaceful Atom*.[62] But he continued to employ the 'technique of calculated exaggeration'[63] even in works clearly meant to be taken seriously.

A major study of issues in human ecology, published in 1970, opens dramatically with the statement: 'The explosive growth of the human population is the most significant terrestrial event of the past million millenia.'[64]

Armed with weapons as diverse as thermonuclear bombs and DDT, this mass of humanity now threatens to destroy most of the life on the planet. Mankind itself may stand on the brink of extinction; in its death throes it could take with it most of the other passengers of Spaceship Earth.[65]

The argument naturally leads Ehrlich to conclude that 'the GNP cannot grow forever'.[66] There are direct quotes or echoes of all the major antagonists of economic growth. 'As John Kenneth Galbraith points out in *The New Industrial State*, it would be entirely logical to set limits on the amount of product a nation needs.'[67] 'Economist K.C. Boulding has begun to develop an exciting set of economic concepts..."cowboy economy"..."space economy".'[68] Like Mishan, Ehrlich deplores the fact that, 'by making the fundamental error of basing our standard of progress on expansion of GNP, we have created a vast industrial complex, and great mental, moral and aesthetic poverty'.[69] Like Marcuse, he believes that the developed countries 'require far too large a slice of the world's resources to maintain our way of life. We, in short, are not developed, we are *overdeveloped*'.[70] Indeed, he considers it 'highly unlikely that the problem of the depletion of non-renewable resources would permit more than a very limited industrial development of most UDCs [underdeveloped countries], unless, of course, there were some sort of massive de-industrialization of most DCs'.[71] Like Marcuse, he is tempted to put his faith in the young rebels of the counterculture:

> In the United States, the unorthodox but constructive and quasi-religious attitudes expressed by members of the so-called 'New Left' and the 'hippie' movements may well save the environment... The members of both these groups of young people share a disdain for material things, a fascination for nature, and an interest in what might be called an ecological way of life.[72]

From the United States, prophecy of doom quickly spread to other western countries. In Britain, the editor of *The Ecologist* published a 'Blueprint for Survival' by a group of eminent British scientists (including five Fellows of the Royal Society)[73] and edited a volume, *Can Britain Survive?*[74] His own conclusions closely paralleled Ehrlich's. 'A serious world food shortage appears inevitable... [The Green Revolution] is extremely unlikely to prove successful.' Britain will not be spared — because 'who will sell [food] to us?' — and cannot hope to feed itself.

We are likely to run out of many of the essential inputs such as arable land, water, minerals and power. In addition we must expect diminishing returns and eventually negative returns on the technological inputs...pesticides, fertilizers, antibiotics... A further condition for the survival of our industrial society is the availability of the required raw materials. This, as we approach the turn of the century, is extremely unlikely... The world's mineral resources are nearing exhaustion. By the end of the century there will be practically no tungsten, copper, lead, zinc, tin, gold, silver or platinum... In the next 30 years we can expect a number of serious ecological disasters. It is possible, for instance, that the Baltic Sea, the Mediterranean and the Black Sea will, before the end of the century, have become biological deserts devoid of any fish life... The conditions for the reappearance of large-scale epidemics are rapidly becoming more and more favourable...germs are rapidly becoming more resistant to antibiotics... There is bound to be increasing disenchantment with modern medicine... As ever less consumer products become available to an ever-increasing population...[75]

Enough to make anyone's flesh creep.

In 1972, the prophets of doom received formidable endorsement from a source with the highest academic and international credentials in the form of a report on *The Limits to Growth*, commissioned by the Club of Rome and prepared by a team of scientists at the Massachusetts Institute of Technology.[76] The Club of Rome, a group of some seventy internationally known public men, was founded in 1968 by an Italian management consultant, Aurelio Peccei, who had already published a book, *The Chasm Ahead* (in which, ironically, he worried about the growing technological gap between the USA and Europe and saw in 'sustained development of the industrial countries' a prerequisite to a solution of the world's problems).[77] He persuaded the Club of Rome to undertake a major research project on what he called the 'predicament of mankind', invited Professor Jay Forrester of MIT to meet the Club in Berne in 1970 and, at Forrester's suggestion, commissioned a group at MIT under the leadership of his co-worker, Dennis L. Meadows, to prepare a report using Forrester's 'world dynamics' model. Funds were obtained from the Volkswagen Foundation, and the report was published in 1972. It received immense publicity and provoked sustained controversy.[78]

Forrester, a distinguished scientist who had made major contributions to the development of digital computers and servomechanisms, had invented what he called a 'system dynamics' approach to the solution of managerial and industrial problems. From an application to industry he had recently extended the approach to urban problems.[79] In response to the invitation by the Club of Rome, he began work in 1970 on equations for a world dynamics model. The outcome, published as *World Dynamics* in 1971, contained all the analytical concepts of *The Limits to Growth*, but virtually no figures. The main contribution of the Meadows team was to put flesh on the analytical skeleton by assembling, in remarkably short time, and feeding into the computer, a vast array of statistics.[80]

The central proposition of Forrester's book was that 'man throughout history has focused on growth — growth in population, standard of living, and geographical boundaries. But in the fixed space of the world, growth must in time give way to equilibrium'.[81] The Meadows study expanded this general proposition into two specific conclusions:

> 1. If the present growth trends in world population, industrialization, pollution, food production, and resource depletion continue unchanged, the limits to growth on this planet will be reached sometime within the next one hundred years. The most probable result will be a rather sudden and uncontrollable decline in both population and industrial capacity. 2. It is possible to alter these growth trends and to establish a condition of ecological and economic stability that is sustainable far into the future. The state of global equilibrium could be designed so that the basic material needs of each person are satisfied and each person has an equal opportunity to realize his individual human potential.[82]

As many commentators on the Forrester–Meadows model pointed out, there was nothing surprising about their conclusions.

> If one starts, as Forrester does, with fixed assumptions about exponential growth, it is apparent that the world is headed for imminent disaster from overcrowding, pollution or exhaustion of natural resources. Moreover, the notion that the only way to stabilise the system is to limit industrialisation, given the premise that pollution and exhaustion of resources are both made directly dependent on industrialisation, is not surprising.[83]

'One gets out of computer models what one puts in.'[84]

Specifically, critics pointed out two fundamental flaws in the Forrester–Meadows analysis. First, it is misleading to speak of resources being 'finite' in physical terms. Investment of capital and advances in technology have throughout history created new resources. 'Once an exponentially improving technology is admitted into the model, along with exponentially growing production, the nature of its outcome changes sharply. The inevitability of crisis when a limit is reached disappears, since the "limits" themselves are no longer fixed, but grow exponentially too.'[85] Secondly, the model contains no adjustment mechanisms of any kind, past behaviour of the major variables being extrapolated unchangingly into the future. Failure to take into account stabilising feedbacks through the price mechanism and through socio-political action largely accounts for the instability of the model. We shall return to some of these aspects of the model, and to other criticisms of *The Limits to Growth*, in the next chapter.

The question may still be asked why scientists such as Forrester and Meadows, without any apparent basis in new empirical evidence, came in 1970 to revive the pessimistic conclusions reached, on very much the same reasoning, by Malthus and Ricardo 150 years earlier. The answer, as one commentator pointed out, is that their conclusions followed from their assumptions and their assumptions were 'very much a reflection of their generally pessimistic view of the world'.[86] With data for many crucial variables as poor as those at the disposal of the Meadows team, 'it is all too easy for a systematic bias reflecting a particularly pessimistic (or for that matter optimistic) view to influence the actual estimates used... The results of the models can be changed radically by altering a few of the principal assumptions'.[87] Viewed in this light, the more extreme predictions of Forrester–Meadows, Ehrlich and other ecologists are seen to have had little to do with science and to have been very much part of the intellectual mood of disillusion about material progress and revolt against the existing social order in the west in the latter 1960s which have been described in the last two chapters. 'The pessimistic ecologist's case fits well with this change in outlook since it confirms the suspicions so many people have of the negative effects of unrestrained growth.'[88] How much this interpretation explains is best illustrated by what the ecologists expected to be the political and social consequences of their prognoses.

The Landing

There was surprisingly little careful analysis of the likely political and social problems of the 'ecological transition' from a growing to a stationary economy, the problem of 'The Landing' — as contrasted with Rostow's 'Take-Off' — as it has cleverly been called.[89] Indeed, there was a tendency among some ecologists to dismiss in rather cavalier fashion 'such specious arguments as the loss of jobs, the lowering of living standards and the raising of prices' with which their critics were 'endeavouring to turn the citizen away from those who are striving to save a viable environment for future generations'.[90] But all the major protagonists expressed strong political sentiments about the present and the future.

Ehrlich's politics, as we have already seen, was close to that of the 'New Left'. Capitalist greed, he thought, bore much of the blame for the state of the western world. 'Profits must obviously be maximized in the short run. Indeed Western Society is in the process of completing the rape and murder of the planet for economic gain.'[91] Like others on the New Left, Ehrlich thought the link between income and work would need to be severed.

> If industrialization of the entire world is neither possible nor desirable, new standards of values will have to be established which will permit *all* peoples to have access to the basic human needs of adequate food, shelter, clothing, education and medical care, regardless of the economic value of their productivity.[92]

His Positive Program, therefore, agreed with Marcuse's in its objectives — de-development of the United States, a 'low-consumption economy of stability and an economy in which there is much more equitable distribution of wealth' — though Marcuse would hardly have shared Ehrlich's touching faith that 'economists' could 'design' such an economy.[93] At the same time, Ehrlich was careful to dissociate himself from the nihilism of some of the New Left: 'The world cannot, in its present critical state, be saved by merely tearing down old institutions.'[94]

Like Forrester and Meadows, Ehrlich recognised that an end to economic growth had very different implications for rich and poor countries. While, as we have seen, he did not think depletion of non-renewable resources would permit more than a very limited industrial development of most less developed countries, he thought there was a moral obligation on the rich countries not only to de-develop themselves but also to offer to help the LDCs to 'semi-develop — not in our image but in whatever image is most appropriate to your culture' — where semi-development meant chiefly 'ecologically sound agricultural development rather than industrialization'.[95] It is not surprising that spokesmen of the less developed countries have been unenthusiastic about the environmentalist movement. They have tended to argue that, in their countries, 'the chief form of pollution is poverty' and have, not entirely without justification, feared that 'they would bear the brunt of any attempt on the part of Western nations to solve the world's ecological problems'.[96] Among the principles they put forward at the 1972 Stockholm Conference was one which stated that 'the environmental policies of all States should enhance and not adversely affect the present or future development potential of developing countries'.[97]

The egalitarian objective was common to all the more prominent American prophets of doom. Some expected an increased risk of social conflict. Even if growth slowed down gradually, rather than ending cataclysmically as in the Forrester–Meadows model, 'the economic and social implications of the steady state are enormous and revolutionary... For several reasons, the important issue of the steady state will be distribution, not production. The problem of relative shares can no longer be avoided by appeals to growth'.[98] But the egalitarian solution is inescapable. 'How will [income] be distributed, if not according to some ethical norm of equality? The steady state would make fewer demands on our environmental resources, but much greater demands on our moral resources.'[99]

The authors of *The Limits to Growth* were more optimistic. Convinced that growth, or at any rate population growth, is itself 'the greatest possible impediment to more equal distribution of the world's resources', they saw it as a positive advantage of the inevitable cessation of growth that it would remove one barrier to equal distribution. 'In a long-term equilibrium state, the relative levels of population and capital, and their relationships to fixed constraints such as land, fresh water, and mineral resources, would have to be set so that there would be enough food and material production to maintain everyone at (at least) a subsistence level.'[100] They conceded that there was 'no assurance that humanity's moral resources would be sufficient to solve the problem of income distribution, even in an equilibrium state'.[101] But some of them, at least, foresaw a Golden Age. In a section with this head-ing, which appears to have formed part of the original draft but was subsequently published separately, two of the authors wrote:

> The presence of global equilibrium could permit the development of an unprecedented golden age for humanity. Freedom from the pressures of providing for ever-increasing numbers of people would make it possible to put substantial effort into the self-realization and development of the individual. Instead of struggling merely to keep alive, human energy could be employed in developing human culture,

and they quoted with approval J.S. Mill's insistence that the stationary state would be 'no stationary state of human improvement' since there would be 'as much scope as ever for human culture'.[102] 'In common with other chiliasts,' as one commentator has observed,

> the new scientific chiliasts are utopians at heart... This is not to denigrate the beliefs of the Forrester/Meadows school in any sense; rather, it is to suggest that they, too, despite the surface appearance of scientific neutrality and objectivity, bring us a message which can only be fully understood in the context of their own beliefs, values, assumptions and goals.[103]

Curiously, the most prominent British prophets of doom did not share the New Left leanings of their American colleagues. The ideal of the eminent scientists who prepared *Blueprint for Survival*, it has been pointed out, was 'quasi-Arcadian, the small town set in the countryside';[104] and the editor of *The Ecologist* who published the manifesto looked forward, in the English conservative romantic tradition of William Morris, Edward Bellamy and Hilaire Belloc, to 'a gradual return to traditional methods of husbandry, which means smaller farms' in agriculture and to 'craftsmanship' in industry.[105] His fears of the serious social consequences of continued economic growth were the fears shared by most pessimistic English conservatives: 'Social disintegration which in turn must increase the need for all types of state intervention — bureaucratic control, police action, state welfare — all of which inevitably give rise to further disintegration.'[106] In one respect he, too, agreed with Marcuse. This was his fear that 'the industrial working classes...will tend to regard conservation as a conspiracy to deprive them of the benefits of our industrial society already reaped by the middle classes who form the bulk of the conservationist movement'.[107] Like the philosopher Passmore,[108] and like Ehrlich in the United States,[109] he expected the environmentalist attack on economic growth to become the chief issue between political parties in western democracies in the 1970s. But the working classes would be on the wrong side: 'Eventually there may well be a new political alignment with no-growth conservationists on the one hand and a growth-oriented alliance between big business interests and trade unions on the other.'[110]

Too much should not be made of the contrast between the American and British ecologists' political outlook. No doubt there were temperamental and ideological conservatives among the American prophets of doom and radicals among the British. The point is that their pessimistic forecasts of the future in large measure reflected their discontent with the present.

Within a few years after the publication of *The Limits to Growth* the 'doomsday syndrome' of which the MIT study was the classic formulation was largely discredited. But the environmentalist case concerning the costs of economic growth in terms of the quality of life had made a deep and lasting impact on public opinion in all western countries and the prophets of doom had given wide currency to the notion, for what it was worth, that economic growth must end 'sooner or later'. In both ways the attacks on economic growth by the critics and revolutionaries had received strong reinforcement.

References

1 Quoted in R. Theobald, 'Needed: A New Development Philosophy', *International Development Review*, March 1964, p. 22.

2 H.J. Barnett and Chandler Morse, *Scarcity and Growth: The Economics of Natural Resource Availability* (Resources for the Future, Johns Hopkins Press, Baltimore, 1963), pp. 7, 10.

3 S.T. Dana, 'Pioneers and Principles', in H. Jarrett (ed.), *Perspectives on Conservation* (Resources for the Future, Johns Hopkins Press, Baltimore, 1958), p. 25.

4 T.B. Nolan, 'The Inexhaustible Resource of Technology', *ibid.*, pp. 51 ff.

5 *Ibid.*, p. 54.

6 J.K. Galbraith, 'How Much Should a Country Consume?', *ibid.*, p. 92.

7 The President's Materials Policy Commission, *Resources for Freedom* (5 volumes, US Government Printing Office, Washington, June 1952).

8 *Ibid.*, vol. 1, p. 1.

9 *Ibid.*, p. 17.

10 *Ibid.*, p. 171.

11 Barnett and Morse, *op. cit.*, p. iv.

12 Cf. L.E. di Marco (ed.), *International Economics and Development*: *Essays in Honor of Raul Prebisch* (Academic Press, New York, 1972).

13 Nolan, *op. cit.*, p. 54.

14 J.J. Spengler (ed.), *Natural Resources and Economic Growth* (Resources for the Future, Washington, 1961), p. 277.

15 *Ibid.*, p. 278.

16 H. Jarrett (ed.), *Environmental Quality in a Growing Economy* (Resources for the Future, Johns Hopkins Press, Baltimore, 1966), p. vii.

17 John Maddox, 'The Doomsday Syndrome', *Saturday Review*, 21 October 1972, reprinted in *Growth and Its Implications for the Future* (Hearings with Appendix, Subcommittee on Fisheries and Wildlife Conservation and the Environment, Committee on Merchant Marine and Fisheries, House of Representatives, US Congress, US Government Printer, Washington, 1973), p. 419 (hereafter cited as *US Congress Hearings*, 1973).

18 T.C. Sinclair, 'Environmentalism: A la recherche du temps perdu — bien perdu?', in H.S.D. Cole et al. (eds), *Thinking about the Future*: *A Critique of The Limits to Growth* (Science Policy Research Unit, Sussex University, Chatto & Windus, London, 1973), p. 180.

19 Barry Commoner, *The Closing Circle*: *Confronting the Environmental Crisis* (Jonathan Cape, London, 1972), p. 69.

20 L.K. Caldwell, *Man and His Environment*: *Policy and Administration* (Harper & Row, New York, 1975), p. 26.

21 T.R. Detwyler (ed.), *Man's Impact on Environment* (McGraw Hill, New York, 1971), p. 4.

22 John Passmore, *Man's Responsibility for Nature* (Duckworth, London, 1974), p. 13.

23 Quoted *ibid.*, pp. 23–4.

24 Commoner, *op. cit.*, p. 255.

25 *Ibid.*, p. 141.

26 Jarrett, *op. cit.* (1966), pp. ix–x.

27 K.E. Boulding, 'Environmental Pollution: Economics and Policy: Discussion', *AEA Proceedings*, May 1971, p. 167.

28 L.C. Cole, 'Thermal Pollution', *BioScience*, vol. 19, 1969, reprinted in Detwyler, *op. cit.*, p. 217.

29 Commoner, *op. cit.*, p. 294.

30 Cf., e.g., E.J. Mishan, 'The Postwar Literature on Externalities: An Interpretative Essay', *Journal of Economic Literature*, March 1971; R. and N.S. Dorfman (eds), *Economics of the Environment* (Norton, New York, 1972); P.A. Victor, *Economics of Pollution* (Macmillan, London, 1972); H.G. Johnson, 'Man and his Environment', *Osaka Economic Papers*, March 1974.

31 Jarrett, *op. cit.* (1966), p. xii.

32 Sinclair, *op. cit.*, p. 184.

33 Caldwell, *op. cit.*, p. 30.

34 *Ibid.*, p. 104.

35 Cf., e.g., W. Beckerman, *In Defence of Economic Growth* (Jonathan Cape, London, 1974), p. 125.

36 Sinclair, *op. cit.*, p. 187.

37 Beckerman, *op. cit.*, p. 116.

38 Sinclair, *op. cit.*, p. 188.

39 *Ibid.*, p. 190.

40 Galbraith, *op. cit.*, pp. 90, 92.

41 *Ibid.*, p. 95.

42 *Ibid.*, p. 96.

43 *Ibid.*, p. 99.

44 *Ibid.*, p. 98.

45 P.M. Hauser, 'The Crucial Value Problems', in Jarrett, *op. cit.* (1958), p. 104.

46 Speech to Nineteenth Session of UN Assembly, 1323rd Plenary Meeting, p. 15, *Official Records of the General Assembly* (United Nations, New York, 1966).

47 Barbara Ward, *Space Ship Earth* (Hamish Hamilton, London, 1966). Barbara Ward thought she had borrowed the idea from the architect Buckminster Fuller (*ibid.*, p. 17). No reference to its use by Fuller has been found before 1969, but he may well have been the originator.

48 *Ibid.*, p. 17.

49 K.E. Boulding, 'The Economics of the Coming Spaceship Earth', in Jarrett, *op. cit.* (1966).

50 *Ibid.*, p. 9.

51 *Ibid.*, p. 7.

52 *Ibid.*, p. 10.

53 *Ibid.*

54 H.E. Daly (ed.), *Toward a Steady-State Economy* (W.H. Freeman & Co., San Francisco, 1973), pp. 14, 16.

55 *Ibid.*, p. 17.

56 K.E. Boulding, 'Environmental Pollution: Economics and Policy: Discussion', *AEA Proceedings*, May 1971, p. 167.

57 Daly, *op. cit.*, p. 6.

58 J. Maddox, *The Doomsday Syndrome* (Macmillan, London, 1972).

59 Paul Ehrlich, *The Population Bomb* (Ballantine, New York, 1968).

60 Paul Ehrlich, 'Eco-Catastrophe!', *Ramparts*, September 1969, reprinted in G. de Bell (ed.), *The Environmental Handbook* (Ballantine, New York, 1970).

61 *Ibid.*, pp. 161 ff.

62 *Ibid.*, p. iii.

63 Maddox, 'The Doomsday Syndrome', *US Congress Hearings*, 1973, p. 420.

64 P.R. and A.H. Ehrlich, *Population Resources Environment: Issues in Human Ecology* (W.H. Freeman & Co., San Francisco, 1970), p. 1.

65 *Ibid.*

66 *Ibid.*, p. 282.

67 *Ibid.*

68 *Ibid.*

69 *Ibid.*, p. 304.

70 *Ibid.*

71 *Ibid.*, p. 300.

72 *Ibid.*, p. 262

73 'A Blueprint for Survival', *The Ecologist*, January 1972, reprinted in *US Congress Hearings*, 1973, pp. 329 ff.

74 E. Goldsmith (ed.), *Can Britain Survive?* (Tom Stacey, London, 1971).

75 *Ibid.*, pp. 244 ff.

76 D.H. Meadows et al., *The Limits to Growth* (Universe Books, New York, 1972).

77 Cf. H. Simmons, 'System Dynamics and Technocracy', in H.S.D. Cole, *op. cit.*, p. 205.

78 See especially *US Congress Hearings*, 1973, which in an appendix of several hundred pages contains the most important contributions to the debate up to 1973; cf. also H.S.D. Cole, *op. cit.*; J. Maddox, *The Doomsday Syndrome*; Beckerman, *op. cit.*; Passmore, *op. cit.*; and references given in these.

79 Simmons, *op. cit.*, pp. 194 ff.

80 Jay W. Forrester, *World Dynamics* (Wright-Allen, Cambridge, 1971); Meadows, *op. cit.*

81 Forrester, *op. cit.*, p. viii.

82 Meadows, *op. cit.*, p. 23.

83 Simmons, *op. cit.*, p. 198.

84 *Ibid.*, p. 197.

85 Carl Kaysen, 'The Computer that Printed out W*O*L*F*', *Foreign Affairs*, Summer 1972, reprinted in *US Congress Hearings*, 1973, p. 189.

86 H.S.D. Cole and R.C. Curnow, 'An Evaluation of the World Models', in H.S.D. Cole, *op. cit.*, p. 133.

87 *Ibid.*

88 Simmons, *op. cit.*, p. 204.

89 J.P. Powelson, *Institutions of Economic Growth: A Theory of Conflict Management in Developing Countries* (Princeton University Press, Princeton, N.J., 1972).

90 Denis Puleston, 'Protecting the Environment', *New Scientist*, 28 September 1972, quoted in Passmore, *op. cit.*, p. 191.

91 P. Ehrlich, in de Bell, *op. cit.*, p. 175.

92 P.R. and A.H. Ehrlich, *op. cit.*, p. 302.

93 *Ibid.*, p. 322.

94 *Ibid.*, pp. 323–4.

95 *Ibid.*, pp. 304–5.

96 Passmore, *op. cit.*, p. 192.

97 Quoted *ibid.*

98 Daly, *op. cit.*, p. 19.

99 *Ibid.*

100 Meadows, *op. cit.*, pp. 178–9.

101 *Ibid.*, p. 179.

102 J. Randers and D.H. Meadows, 'The Carrying Capacity of the Global Environment: A Look at the Ethical Alternatives', in D.L. and D.H. Meadows (eds), *Toward Global Equilibrium: Collected Papers* (Wright-Allen, Cambridge, Mass., 1973), p. 335.

103 Simmons, *op. cit.*, p. 207.

104 Passmore, *op. cit.*, p. 52.

105 Goldsmith, *op. cit.*, p. 246.

106 *Ibid.*, p. 249.

107 *Ibid.*, p. 250.

108 See ch. 7, p. 95.

109 P.R. and A.H. Ehrlich, *op. cit.*, p. 291.

110 Goldsmith, *op. cit.*, p. 251.

10 Assessment

The purpose of the preceding chapters has been to explain the rise and fall of economic growth; how and why, within little more than two decades, economic growth came to be first elevated to the front rank among objectives of national policy in western countries and then widely denigrated and notably demoted. This done, the reader, adequately provoked and perhaps stimulated, might be left to draw his own conclusions. But there is a temptation and, so one is told, an obligation to say a little more. Hence these concluding reflections on the issues under debate, an attempt to assess where it leaves us on economic growth as a policy objective.

The Possibility of Economic Growth

About the possibility of continued economic growth little need be added to what was said at the end of the last chapter. The one indubitably valid point made by the prophets of doom, that current rates of growth of population and per capita income cannot be maintained indefinitely, was neither new nor in itself very interesting. That man will not survive on earth for all time has long been known as a strong probability. If doom is millenia off, the responsibility of the present to the nth future generation is a fine point in moral philosophy. 'Why', as Arthur Lewis asked, 'should we stay poor so that the life of the human race may in some centuries to come be extended for a further century or so?'[1]

The interesting question is whether there are good reasons to fear that growth of per capita income, superimposed upon population growth, will outrun available resources in the near or foreseeable future. Neo-Malthusian cries of alarm that this or that natural resource will *soon* run out have been raised at intervals, and been disproved by events, ever since Malthus. The version to which the Club of Rome lent its name is unlikely to prove an exception.

The Forrester–Meadows forecasts of the time it would take before exponential growth would exhaust finite reserves of various resources involved two fallacies. One was Malthus's own failure to make adequate allowance for technical progress as an offset to diminishing returns. 'Once an exponentially improving technology is admitted into the model...the inevitability of crisis...disappears.'[2] The other, more fundamental, fallacy lay in the very concept, meaningless to an economist, of 'finite' resources. The higher the price of any mineral or other natural resource, the larger is the volume of (lower-grade, less accessible) reserves which it is economic to exploit and therefore the larger the world's total known reserves for economic purposes. A quite modest rise in the current world price of uranium, for example, would make it economic to extract uranium from sea water; what then are the world's 'finite' reserves of uranium? A higher price also encourages economy in use and development of substitutes, thus reducing demand, and stimulates exploration and technological advance in mining and processing, thus increasing supply.

It is most unlikely that the world will ever 'run out' of any natural resource, in the sense that suddenly there will be none left. Rather, if and to the extent that, with population and economic growth, demand for any resource, such as petroleum, runs ahead of supply, its price will tend to rise. This, if it happens to essential materials for which no substitutes are available, will in itself tend to slow down economic growth. The only questions for economic policy, that is for government intervention, posed by the neo-Malthusians of the 1970s are, first, whether there are reasons to fear that the forces of the market will not operate effectively to maintain balance between world supply and demand and, second, whether price increases of unevenly distributed natural resources may not cause intolerable changes in the distribution of world income. The alacrity with which the OPEC cartel responded to Club-of-Rome-inspired predictions of an energy crisis by raising the price of crude oil and the effects that this had on net oil importing LDCs, such as India, suggests that there is little ground for pessimism about the first of these questions, but a good deal about the second.

Much the same conclusion applies to those natural resources which influence the world's food-producing capacity, though the growth that matters here is in any case that of population rather than of per capita income. There are no technical or economic reasons for doubting that the world's capacity to produce food can grow ahead of the world's needs for food for many generations. Provided the rate of growth of the world's population can, with economic development and family planning programmes in the most populous LDCs, be slowed down towards an annual rate not much above zero within the next half century, there is a good chance that food production will increase sufficiently even on realistic assumptions about the political and institutional obstacles in the way. But the proviso is of course a large one and, given the grossly uneven distribution of food-production capacity relative to food needs among the countries of the world, there are very likely to be threats of increasing malnutrition and periodic famine in the most vulnerable areas.

Aside from exhaustion of non-renewable resources, early limits to economic growth have been predicated on irreversible damage to the environment. On most of these dire predictions, of over-heating of the earth's atmosphere, destruction of the ionosphere and irremediable damage to ecological balance in other forms, the weight of reputable scientific opinion appears to have come down against the prophets of doom.[3] But it is only fair to add that our ignorance about these matters is still great, and the prophets will have done good in making humanity aware of dangers that may need watching.

Like earlier neo-Malthusians, those of the early 1970s will have performed a valuable service in encouraging a more rational attitude to the use of scarce resources, especially condemnation of profligate waste and encouragement of economy through recycling and in other ways. In the short run, however, their greatest impact has probably been to lend powerful support to those forces in the rich western countries which were already making sections of public opinion less enthusiastic about economic growth as a major objective of national policy. Somewhat para-doxically, the chief influence of those who pronounced much further economic growth as impossible was to reinforce those who thought it undesirable. The wish, as so often, was father to the thought.

The Desirability of Economic Growth

'Vanity of vanities', said the preacher more than two thousand years ago. 'What profit hath man of all his labour wherein he laboureth under the sun?' Ever since, wise men have deplored the folly and greed of mankind lusting after earthly possessions, and minorities have taken vows of poverty, entered monasteries or in other ways 'opted out'.

There was therefore nothing altogether new about the questioning of the desirability of economic growth of the 1960s, but it was more vocal and widespread than perhaps ever before. Once again, protest came from two quite distinct quarters, social critics in the tradition of J.S. Mill, on the one side, and radical dissenters of the counterculture, on the other. Both agreed that western society has overrated the benefits and underrated the costs of economic growth, but they agreed on very little else.

The significance of the hippies and other young people who withdrew from affluent society, at least partially and temporarily, and of militant radicals who believed that the first step towards a society better than any yet seen on earth was to tear down the existing one, lay in what they were, symptoms of social malaise, rather than in what they said. But the alienation from the values of western society which they displayed in extreme form affected in some degree a whole generation. It provided a receptive climate for intellectual criticism of growthmanship.

A good deal of this criticism was elitist in the least admirable sense, sometimes comically so. When Mishan and others grumbled about the discomforts one had to put up with, now that almost everybody had motor cars, and about the thoughtless manner in which enchanting spots on the Riviera were being spoiled by mass tourism, they clearly invited Crosland's caustic summary of their protest: 'Affluence is obviously more agreeable when it is a minority condition.'[4]

Even this one-eyed perspective, however, focused on a valid point. Another century of growth of population and per capita income since Mill had changed the scale of many of the problems caused by growth. Millions crowded into conurbations, tens of millions of motor vehicles and countless other products and by-products of industrial civilisation were adversely affecting the quality of life of everyone, not merely of a privileged minority. Clearly, with rising per capita income, the costs of economic growth were, in this sense at least, increasing relative to the benefits.

Some of the critics, of course, went much further. Even if growth had no serious costs, Galbraith seemed to be arguing, what is the point in this ever-swelling affluence? 'The true and genuine needs of man', Schumacher asserted, 'are limited.'[5] Have we not enough? Is further growth satisfying any real wants? Are we caught up in a system in which 'production creates the wants it seeks to satisfy'?[6] How can one justify a society which yields 'the ever rising "standard package" of consumer goods'[7] at the price of 'everything that ultimately matters to the quality of its members' lives'?[8]

Philosopher-kings naturally do not think much of affluence. As philosophers their material wants are modest, and as kings they are usually free of serious financial worries. Ordinary mortals, even in affluent American suburbia, remained unconvinced that Galbraith and Schumacher knew what was enough for them, if only because for most of them the goods and services offered by 'consumerism' provided some of the sources of social status and self-respect which men like Galbraith and Schumacher found more easily in their intellectual pursuits and public standing. And if the critics insisted that, surely, there *must* be a living standard that is high enough for anyone's taste, this seemed almost frivolously irrelevant to the desirability of further economic growth for any foreseeable future. Whatever was enough for the well-to-do in the half dozen richest countries was a great deal more than was enjoyed by the majority even in these countries, let alone by the overwhelming majority of mankind in the poverty-stricken countries of Asia, Africa and Latin America.

Nor was the balance between the benefits and costs of further economic growth as obvious as some of the critics — and some of the advocates — claimed. It may be easy to accept that a second car or a colour TV set is not one of the things that ultimately matter to the quality of men's lives, but much less easy to agree on what does matter. Civilised people tend to romanticise the life of primitive people, lived in the intimacy and affection of the village community, unspoiled by the noise and stench of factories and motor cars, close to nature, unhurried and unworried; they forget the lack of privacy, of individual freedom, of education and literary culture, the tyranny of chiefs and medicine men, the terror of hostile spirits, the short expectation of life. Urban people tend to romanticise the rural life, forgetting what Marx called its 'idiocy',[9] as well as its toil and insecurity. If there is so much room for disagreement on what matters to the quality of life, is it very helpful to declare oneself 'uninterested in economic growth, except where there is clear evidence that...it improves the quality of men's lives'?[10]

Perhaps what really matters has nothing to do with the lives of ordinary people at all but is to be seen in the 'ultimate fruits of civilisation', great works of art and thought which, we are told, are threatened by the pace of contemporary economic advance.[11] Who now cares about the happiness, or even the quality of the lives, of the ordinary people who lived in the China of the Ming dynasty, in Moghul India, ancient Greece or Renaissance Italy? Of course, what we would all like is higher living standards for all *and* great new works of art — and perhaps this is what we are getting. Some of the critics of the philistinism of affluent contemporary society, *laudatores temporis acti,* might be reminded that most artistic innovators, from Beethoven to Stravinsky, from Turner to Matisse and Picasso, were initially rejected by their contemporaries as offensive to all canons of good taste. But if and in so far as there is a conflict between material and cultural progress, this may not be a conflict that can be resolved by a more judicious trade-off — more culture for less growth. We shall return to this question in a moment.

In any case, it is evident all around that economic growth, the ever-rising standard package of consumer goods, does not *guarantee* happiness. Arthur Lewis, as we saw, argued that

> what distinguishes men from pigs is that men have greater control over their environment; not that they are more happy. And on this test, economic growth is greatly to be desired. The case for economic growth is that it gives man greater control over his environment, and thereby increases his freedom.[12]

This argument, which is still very persuasive in relation to the majority in the very poor countries, may not now carry much conviction in relation to growth in the not so poor countries. Even for the majority in these countries, however, to be deprived of substantial parts of the available package of consumer goods and services is, quite evidently, a major source of unhappiness.

Rightly or wrongly, ordinary mortals want higher living standards than they happen to have and, as the clash of competing income claims of which accelerating inflation may be a symptom shows, fight bitterly for them, not only in the form of higher wages and salaries to buy more goods and services for personal consumption, but also for higher standards of government services in education, health, social security, transport, housing and much else. Those who object that these are merely habits inculcated by a pernicious capitalist system may be reminded that similar habits were condemned by Old Testament prophets and are reported to be reasserting themselves in the Soviet Union and other socialist countries. A desire for improvement in material living standards appears to be a trait of human nature which shows itself whenever the possibility of such improvement emerges and so long as it is not sublimated by religious or ideological fervour or repressed by the forces of an authoritarian state.

This is not in itself evidence of the desirability of a high rate of economic growth, and therefore of policies which more or less effectually pursue it as a high-priority objective, although it may be a reason for doubt whether the majority of one's fellow men can be persuaded to downgrade it. But there are, as we noted before, other considerations that need to be weighed in the scales for and against economic growth.[13] At least three incidental but important advantages have been claimed for a growing over a stationary economy. Economic growth eases problems of structural change and adjustment; it softens the struggle over shares between interest groups; and it is a necessary condition of full employment in a private enterprise economy.

There can be little doubt about the first. It is not remotely realistic to imagine humanity reverting to the changeless existence of a Pacific island idyll in which problems of change of technology, of supply and demand, just do not arise; and when they do, they are more easily accommodated in a growing than in a stationary economy. The second is more debatable; it is valid in so far as the struggle over shares of income and wealth springs from a desire of individuals and groups to improve their absolute condition, but not if their concern is with their relative position in the social scale, and there is much evidence of the latter type of motivation in the world around us.[14] The third claim, which derives support from both the Harrod–Domar thesis and from Schumpeter's view of capitalist economic development, is of course specific to a particular economic system — forced labour or making unemployment illegal would quickly dispose of it — but it implies that slower or zero economic growth may have a high price to those who prefer a capitalist market economy to the available alternatives.

Considering the extent of the anti-growth literature of the past decade, it is curious how little effort has been made to visualise the cultural implications of a slowing down of economic growth towards zero in the existing national economies, capitalist or socialist. J.S. Mill was quite confident that a stationary economy would be 'no stationary state of human improvement', that there would be 'as much scope as ever for all kinds of mental culture, and moral and social progress'.[15] Yet it is not easy to imagine the culture of a stationary society, without capital accumulation and without technical progress. Not that we are without precedents. On the contrary, as Keynes pointed out, it is in just such stationary conditions, or nearly so, that mankind lived 'from the earliest times of which we have record...down to the beginning of the eighteenth century';[16] and that long stretch of history certainly saw the emergence of great civilisations and flourishing culture — in China, Egypt, India, Renaissance Italy, Elizabethan England, to name but a few. But all these were aristocratic civilisations whose culture was the creation and prerogative of a small elite; their economic foundations were in slavery, serfdom or at best a life of toil and bare subsistence for the masses of the people who for the most part could not conceive of a better life on earth and found resignation and perhaps consolation in religion. They were also all civilisations which predated the possibility of sustained material progress for the ordinary man that came, slowly over centuries, following the emergence of rational enquiry, science and technology in Renaissance Europe.

People did not begin to think of material progress as desirable until events proved that it was possible. Will people cease to think economic growth desirable so long as it remains possible, physically and economically? Can mankind, having eaten of the tree of knowledge, be expected to revert voluntarily to the stage of pre-scientific innocence? Of course, most of the critics today envisage, in the first instance, a mere slowing down, not a cessation, of economic growth. But Mill's formulation in terms of a stationary economy usefully sharpens the issue. The nagging doubts which his optimism quite fails to allay revolve around two questions. The first is whether culture can flourish within constraints imposed on economic advance, and by necessary implication on the pursuit of science and technology, by a conscious national policy of zero economic growth. And secondly, even if this could be imagined, whether voters in rich democracies can be persuaded to adopt such a national policy. This is not to say that it would be impossible to halt economic growth. But might not the transition to a stationary economy require a powerful Stalinesque state which tells people that they may not have the motor cars they want, or a Maoist one which ensures that they do not want the cars they may not have? And what sort of culture will flourish in either?

It was a sound insight that led the high priest of the contemporary anti-growth movement, Mishan, to see the root of all evil in 'Science — without social conscience or social purpose — like some ponderous multi-purpose robot that is powered by its own insatiable curiosity'.[17] His contemporary, Simone de Beauvoir, came to much the same conclusion when she asked: 'When had the decline begun? The dry knowledge was preferred to wisdom and mere usefulness to beauty. Along with the Renaissance, rationalism, capitalism and the worship of science.'[18]

One other of J.S. Mill's comments on economic growth is relevant: 'For the safety of national independence it is essential that a country should not fall much behind its neighbours in these things.'[19] We noted in an earlier chapter how important a part cold war rivalry played in promoting economic growth as a national objective in the United States. In part, of course, defence expenditure competes for resources with personal consumption and other objects of government spending. But in the longer run, the military power of a modern national state is believed to depend on its overall productive capacity, as well as its industrial and technological potential. This is bound to remain a powerful obstacle to the adoption of a deliberate policy of slowing down economic growth in any one major country unless it can be done by international agreement. Compared with the task facing negotiators in Economic Growth Limitations Talks, SALT was child's play.

Four conclusions would seem to emerge from these cursory reflections on the debate over the possibility and desirability of continued economic growth.

First, there is little if any convincing scientific evidence that exhaustion of non-renewable natural resources or irreversible damage to the biosphere will set early limits to growth, though it is possible, but by no means certain, that economic growth will be slowed down over the next century by rising long-run cost curves for some key resources, such as fossil fuels. (Much here turns on the prospects for decline in the rate of growth of the world's population, but these depend chiefly on what happens in the less developed countries of Asia, Africa and South America; they are not directly relevant to the issue of economic growth in the sense of growth of per capita income.)

Second, as per capita income rises, the costs of economic growth tend to increase relative to its benefits; it is clearly sensible to limit these costs, in terms of damage to the environment and the social problems of life in urban and industrial society, if necessary by paying the price of a slower rate of economic growth, and voters in developed democracies can almost certainly be made to understand and accept this.

But, third, whether or not 'enough' is in principle definable and however wise men may shake their heads or tear their hair over the folly of mankind, there does not seem to be the least chance that people will voluntarily forgo opportunities for higher standards of living, whether in the form of higher personal consumption or of public services, merely because enough is enough. The pressures for the highest possible rate of economic growth, in the sense of the highest rate for which the benefits to the public at large or to influential groups are not demonstrably outweighed by the costs, will go on, with fear in major countries lest their country 'fall much behind its neighbours in these things' as merely added reinforcement.

Therefore, fourth, the realistic question to ask is not whether further economic growth is possible or desirable, or even how rapid it should be, but what *kind* of growth we should aim at. To have focused public attention on this question is the major achievement of the critique of economic growth of the past decade.

The Right Kind of Economic Growth

The public men, politicians, economists and others, who in western countries in the years after the Second World War proclaimed the importance of attaining a high rate of economic growth were neither ignorant nor stupid nor evil. They did not ignore, or dismiss as unimportant, problems of poverty and an equitable distribution of income, problems of conservation of natural resources and protection of the environment, improvement in standards of education, health and other public services, or of conditions of work and living in industrial cities. They believed that all these problems could be solved or alleviated more easily if the capacity to produce goods and services for all these purposes was increased year by year through economic growth. They assumed, for instance, that the problem of poverty could be reduced, even without any changes in the distribution of income, by economic growth which would make all better off, and that a more equal distribution of income could be achieved more easily in a rapidly growing economy in which some could be made better off without anyone being made worse off.

It is therefore a mistake to imagine that anyone wanted economic growth 'for its own sake' or was after 'mere GNP'. Certainly, some expressions of growthmanship went to absurd lengths, and there was a case for 'dethroning GNP' in the technical sense of trying to find a more adequate statistical measure, or set of measures, of economic welfare. There was also substance in the criticism that single-minded pursuit of economic growth as a major objective of national policy was liable to divert attention from problems which 'mere economic growth' would not resolve, and to bring new problems arising from the external diseconomies or incidental costs of economic growth.

Galbraith was undoubtedly right in pillorying the contrasts between 'private affluence and public squalor', especially though not exclusively in the United States, even if his magisterial assessment of the real wants of other people was naive and his obsession with 'want creation' by wicked advertisers, though not entirely without point, something of a red herring. The capitalist market economy of western democracies has had an inherent bias in favour of private and against public goods, because voters have been much readier to demand public goods than to pay the necessary taxes and because power has been heavily concentrated in the hands of the well-to-do who, in a welfare state with progressive taxation, would have to foot a major part of the bill.

Similarly, the environmentalists were right in drawing attention to the whole range of problems of pollution and other adverse effects on the environment that rapid industrial and urban growth was bringing in its train, even though some screamed so loud to be heard that they stood in danger of discrediting a worthy cause.

Again, social critics were right who pointed out that two decades of unprecedentedly rapid growth were leaving behind pockets of appalling poverty among weak and vulnerable groups even in some of the richest countries, and were widening the gap in living standards between rich and poor countries. In the less developed countries themselves, moreover, the pursuit of economic growth was frequently increasing inequality, without any automatic assurance that the benefits of modernisation which accrued in the first instance to privileged groups would 'trickle down' to the rest, that even high rates of economic growth would bring 'development'.

In all three respects, economic growth, it has become increasingly apparent, is not enough. Deliberate policies are needed to modify the pattern of growth so as to reduce the costs of economic growth and ensure a more equitable distribution of its benefits.

This, however, sounds easier than it may prove to be. When the growthmen of the 1950s and 1960s advocated the highest possible rate of growth of GNP, they knew quite well, at least in their bones, that this 'highest possible' rate was somewhere around 5 to 10 per cent a year, rather than 20 to 25 per cent, because of limits set not so much by available resources and technology but by other desirable objectives, each acting as a constraint on all the others in the necessary policy-mix. The composition of GNP had to be such as to meet the community's demands as expressed in the market or through the ballot box, there had to be a politically acceptable distribution of income, and the policy instruments used had to be consistent with reasonably full employment, stable prices, external balance and with the political framework of western democracies, to mention only some of the more obvious objectives. What the debate over economic growth has achieved is wider recognition that the trade-offs between the objective of a high rate of economic growth and some other objectives need to be reconsidered. The 'highest possible' rate of economic growth still remains a desideratum, but many now think that this rate is lower than had been assumed if sufficient weight is given to some conflicting objectives, such as protection of the environment and of more intangible aspects of the quality of life, and a more equitable distribution of income.

Economic growth as an objective was so popular partly because it was an easy option. In its extreme form, growthmanship was a form of escapism — 'the desire to avoid or blur the unpleasant choices at the margin between different priorities among policy aims'.[20] Many other problems would be more manageable if only we had enough economic growth. By the same token, the critique of economic growth has brought us back face to face with the unpleasant choices. The danger now is that in our anxiety to correct the earlier neglect of equality, the quality of life and the environment, another desideratum, the maintenance of a relatively liberal social order, may be sacrificed.

Compared with the others, the environmental problems seem at this stage relatively the most manageable, formidable as they are.

In most cases of pollution, the adverse effects, once attention is drawn to them, are sufficiently clear and diffused, and the costs of eliminating them or rendering them innocuous sufficiently modest, that electorates in democratic countries will allow governments, and occasionally even push them, to take remedial action. It did not take long to rid London and other English industrial cities of smog and, once the will is there, it does not cost much or take long to clean polluted rivers and lakes, to counteract soil erosion, reafforest denuded forest land and even clear urban slums and traffic congestion. One to 2 per cent of GNP has been estimated as the cost of adequate environmental control in developed countries.[21] This may mean a somewhat slower rate of economic growth as conventionally measured than would otherwise be possible, though it has rightly been argued that GNP as a measure of economic growth is misleading in so far as it fails to take account of social costs such as pollution. It will also mean more government intervention in the processes of the market, both through direct controls where these are the only effective way of preventing serious injury to the public, through taxes and other ways of making polluters pay, and through government action to repair past damage to the natural and urban environment.

What makes most of the other problems so much more intractable is that they involve redistribution, taking from some and giving it to others. To cite the most glaring example, even the poor in the rich countries are, with few exceptions, better off than the majority in the poor countries. Yet, with few exceptions, they will not allow their governments to divert more than a minute fraction of the national income from expenditures which benefit themselves, such as social security or health or roads or defence, towards aid (or aid through trade) to the poorer countries. They regard themselves as entitled to sell at the highest possible prices or keep in the ground the scarce minerals that others may need, to impose a monopoly on the resources of the ocean within 200 miles of their shores, to keep out unwanted immigrants, and generally to look after themselves first. And this applies with quite minor variations as much to well-to-do socialist as to well-to-do capitalist countries, and to the most, vis-a-vis the least, developed countries within the Third World.

The problem of redistribution is marginally easier within than between countries because there are national governments with power to act and because the haves, whether from a sense of social obligation or from considerations of enlightened self-interest, have allowed governments in varying degree to help the have-nots by measures to alleviate the worst poverty and undertake some redistribution of income through the mechanisms of the welfare state. Yet even here, in the domestic arena of the rich countries, the problems are becoming all but unmanageable within the democratic political framework of relatively open societies based on market economies — problems of maintaining full employment, of keeping inflation within bounds, of holding a balance between labour and capital, between rural and urban interests, between regions, between competing demands for the taxpayer's money — all problems involving struggle between warring sections over shares in a limited national product.

In most of the countries of the Second and Third World, all such problems are contained by the concentration of authoritarian state power in the hands of military dictators or party leaders and cadres. Even in the western democracies large sections of public opinion seem ready to trade political democracy, civil liberties and private enterprise for the economic advantages — full employment, stable prices, greater equality of personal income and wealth, and faster economic growth through state planning — which they hope for under socialism.

The right *kind* of economic growth is an objective on which it will be far more difficult to secure agreement than a high *rate* of economic growth, and the slower the target rate of economic growth the more difficult the problem will become. Those who still regard the maintenance of an open society, in which power is diffused and certain freedoms reasonably safeguarded, as worth a high price in terms of most objectives of economic policy, are bound to view the prospect of narrowing limits to economic growth with foreboding. Whether economic growth slows down in western countries because of increasing difficulties of national management of mixed economies, or because of rising costs of environmental controls or because of rising prices of essential raw materials or because of political pressures from the Second and Third World for a 'new international economic order', one consequence is very likely to be an enlargement of the role and power of the state.

To the extent that the demand for the right kind of economic growth becomes a battle cry for equity or even equality it is liable to strain social consensus beyond the limits compatible with a free society. *Fiat iustitia si ruant coeli* is a noble maxim. But the pursuit of justice on earth at any price is indeed only too likely to cause the heavens to fall.

References

1 Quoted in ch. 6, p. 80.

2 C. Kaysen, quoted in ch. 9, p. 133.

3 Cf. W. Beckerman, *In Defence of Economic Growth* (Jonathan Cape, London, 1974), ch. 5.

4 C.A.R. Crosland, *A Social-Democratic Britain* (Fabian Tract No. 404, London, January 1971), reprinted in C.A.R. Crosland, *Socialism Now and Other Essays* (Jonathan Cape, London, 1974), p. 79.

5 Quoted in ch. 7, p. 90.

6 J.K. Galbraith, quoted in ch. 7, p. 87.

7 D. Riesman, quoted in ch. 7, p. 86.

8 D.M. Bensusan-Butt, quoted in ch. 7, p. 89.

9 Quoted in ch. 2, p. 10.

10 J. Passmore, quoted in ch. 7, p. 95.

11 D.M. Bensusan-Butt, quoted in ch. 7, p. 90.

12 Quoted in ch. 6, p. 71.

13 See ch. 6, pp. 72–5.

14 On the implications of the relative income hypothesis, cf. Beckerman, *op. cit.*, p. 96. While this present book was in press, the implications for economic growth as a policy objective of 'positional competition' have been spelled out much more fully in an important and exciting book, Fred Hirsch, *Social Limits to Growth* (Routledge & Kegan Paul, London, 1977); a review article by H.W. Arndt appeared in *Quadrant*, January 1978.

15 J.S. Mill, *Principles of Political Economy* (5th edn, Parker, London, 1862), vol. II, pp. 325–6.

16 Quoted in ch. 2, p. 5.

17 Quoted in ch. 7, p. 92.

18 Simone de Beauvoir, *Les Belles Images* (Penguin, London, 1969), quoted in T.C. Sinclair, 'Environmentalism: A la recherche du temps perdu — bien perdu?', in H.S.D. Cole et al. (eds), *Thinking about the Future: A Critique of The Limits to Growth* (Science Policy Research Unit, Sussex University, Chatto & Windus, London, 1973), p. 178.

19 Quoted in ch. 2, p. 12.

20 D. Winch, quoted in ch. 7, p. 94.

21 Cf. Beckerman, *op. cit.*, pp. 193 ff.

Index of names

Index of subjects